Teach Us to Number Our Days

Teach Us to Number Our Days

DAVID ROPER

DISCOVERY HOUSE
PUBLISHERS®

Feeding the Soul with the Word of God

Discovery House Publishers is affiliated with RBC Ministries, Grand Rapids, Michigan.

Discovery House books are distributed to the trade exclusively by Barbour Publishing, Inc., Uhrichsville, Ohio.

Interior design by Nick Richardson

Library of Congress Cataloging-in-Publication Data
Available upon request.

ISBN: 978-1-57293-196-1

Printed in the United States of America

09 10 11 12 / / 10 9 8 7 6 5 4 3 2

Teach us to number our days aright,
that we may gain a heart of wisdom.

—PSALM 90:12

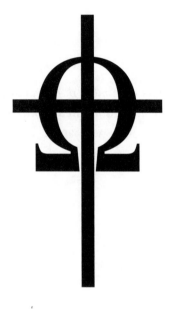

The medieval church adopted the symbol of a cross, super-imposed on an omega, to symbolize Christian aging. The omega (the last letter of the Greek alphabet) reminds us that Christ is at the end of our life. The cross symbolizes His love for us through all our years.

CONTENTS

Contents

. . . .

INTRODUCTION

BOOKS, NOTE CARDS, MEMOS, SHREDS AND SHARDS

Books, note cards, memos, shreds and shards of
some fresh-excavated pile or file;
an hour on this, an hour on that.
—T. M. MOORE

Some years ago I came across William Penn's classic work, *Some Fruits of Retirement*. He wrote in his introduction: "He [Penn] has now had some Time he could call his own; a Property he was never so much Master of before." Having retired from public life, Penn now had more time to report his thoughts on his final years.

Although I'm not retired, my schedule is relaxed these days, and I have more time to call my own—time for reading, reflection, and prayer. These essays are, in part, the fruit of that "retirement."

11

This collection is eclectic in nature, based on things I've seen, experienced, read, or thought about in recent years. They're made up of "memos, shreds and shards" drawn from my journals, letters, e-mails, and a host of jottings that I've sent out to a few friends from time to time.

I write from the perspective of an older person, having crossed the biblical boundary of "three-score and ten years" five years ago. Though more or less "hale and hearty," as they say of old timers, I know I'm living on borrowed time. With Cowper, I want to "close life wisely and not waste my own." I suppose that's why I now feel compelled to pass on these scraps of writing, accompanied by Israel's old-timer's prayer: "Do not forsake me, O God, when I'm old and gray, *until I declare your power to the next generation*, your might to those who are to come."[1]

Yet this is not a book about aging, per se, though I do cover many of the concerns that inhere as we grow older. More than anything else, it's about my own journey toward maturity. In that sense, though in my dotage, I'm still "coming of age."

As I read through these chapters again, in preparation for writing this introduction, it also occurred to me that almost all of them have something to do with the goodness of God. That's to be expected, I suppose, for through the years I truly have "tasted the kindness of the Lord."[2]

Our culture is constantly telling us, in one way or

another, that youth is the time of "wine and roses," but I must disagree. Despite the troubles of old age, and they are many, I must say, with the wedding guests at Cana, that my Lord has saved the best wine for the last. He has touched these final years of my life with delightful sweetness, fragrance and bouquet. With Browning, "Let me attest . . . I have lived, seen God's hand through a lifetime, and all was for the best!"

DAVID ROPER
Boise, Idaho

FORGETFULNESS

If, on leaving the company, a young man cannot
remember where he has left his hat, it is nothing.
But when an old man forgets, everyone says, "Ah,
his memory is going."
—DR. SAMUEL JOHNSON

Lately I find myself forgetting ordinary things on a regular basis. My misfortune manifests itself in a fading recollection of where I left my car keys, my reading glasses, my sunglasses, my hat.

I even forget my best thoughts, which seem to come and go at random; I have little control over them these days. Plato said our minds are like aviaries and our thoughts are like birds. It's an apt metaphor for me. I reach for one thought and frighten it away, then grasp at another that quickly flits away from my mind—unless I write it down.

There are other things I've forgotten, but right now I can't remember what they are.

There's an upside to forgetting, however. There

15

are things I *want* to forget, not the least of which are the things in the past that I could have, should have, done. John Greenleaf Whittier said, "Of all sad words of tongue or pen, the saddest are these: 'It might have been.'" Indeed.

I think of relationships I might have nurtured, projects I should have finished, decisions that were better unmade. And certainly my past behavior has been regrettable. An old acquaintance recently characterized me as "a mean kid" in my youth. It saddens me to think that he remembers me that way. I think of all the things I've "done, and been; the shame / Of motives late revealed, and the awareness / Of things ill done and done to others' harm."[3] I wish I could forget them.

Further, I want to forget the wrongs I've received in my lifetime. It's easy to brood over them and become bitter and resentful, like Charles Dickens's sad, eccentric Miss Havisham, who was jilted at the altar and stopped all the clocks in her house at the hour of her disappointment. Her bitterness was frozen in time. I don't want mine to be.

All of us, I'm sure, have been wronged in some way or another at various times; friends and enemies have dishonored and grieved us. We may cling to bitterness over our childhood and remember old wounds from a parent's hand.

Some rise above it and leave it behind. I once asked a cruelly abused friend how he dealt with his grievances. "I've got a good forgetter," he replied. I wish I could get one too.

All of which encourages me to recall the patriarch Joseph. He, too, had much to forget. He was "a mean kid" too, flaunting his most–favored status, wearing it on his sleeve, so to speak.[4]

Joseph further alienated himself from his family by endlessly relating his dreams—dreams that were true, as it turned out, but which, when repeated over and over, augmented the resentment of his brothers. They "hated him all the more because of his dream and what he had said."[5] Israel's wise men would have called him a *peti*—a young fool.

In his youth, a series of calamitous events cascaded down on Joseph's head, like bricks tumbling out of a dump truck, one after another. He was snatched from his doting father by his brothers, cast into a pit, and passed on to a band of Bedouins who in turn sold him into slavery in Egypt.

In Egypt his life continued to be a series of tragic indignities. He was tempted by a determined seductress who, when spurned, accused him of raping her. He was summarily tried, convicted, imprisoned, and left to languish in isolation for a dozen years or more, forgotten by family and friends.

Yet in the end Joseph's bitterness was transformed into forgiveness and love. He named his firstborn son Manasseh (Hebrew for "caused to forget") for, he said, "God has made me forget all my trouble."[6]

How did God cause him to forget? Did he work some magic on Joseph that erased his memory? No, God taught him to look at his past in a redemptive way: Joseph came to see that God's hand controlled all that he bore. And he knew that God's ways were "perfect."[7]

Two texts underscore that perception: "You *sold* me," Joseph said to his brothers, "but God *sent* me here to preserve life." And again, "You *intended* to harm me, but God *intended* it for good to accomplish what is now being done, the saving of many lives."[8]

Joseph remembered well what his brothers had done: they had sold him into slavery. That injustice and cruelty he could never forget. But behind the bitter experiences of the past he saw the providence of God. This is the mystery of sovereignty: God works through evil to accomplish His will. "He permits evil," Augustine said, "to transform it into good."

The past cannot be changed, but it can be redeemed. It cannot be forgotten *per se* (for some things will never be forgotten), but it can be swallowed up in God's sovereign purposes and left behind.

How can we forget the bitterness of our past? By seeing God's providence in every event of our lives, even in our mistakes and in others' malice. The God of love and wisdom has taken the worst that we have done and is turning it into eternal good. We may not see or know that good until we step into eternity itself, but it is certain—as certain as the lovingkindness of God.

How Does Your Garden Grow?

All Beauty Speaks of Thee.
— EDWARD GRUBB

I received a letter from an old friend some months ago in which she wrote of her daughter and some things they share in common:

> Both of us are loners, enjoying the quiet, thoughtful places in our days . . . both of us [enjoy] devouring words and color, deep friendships, worshiping our Lord, appreciating His gifts . . . and we both like children's stories and outrageous laughter. Her garden is her delight, and it speaks of every part of her character. The first time she really sensed God's presence, many years ago, was in her garden. A memorable time!

As for me, I never cared for gardening when I was younger; it looked too much like work, and I already had too much work to do. Lately, however, I've taken to gardening, though the joke around our place is that flowers come to our house to die. I'm an old man but a very young gardener.

I must say, however, despite my inexperience and ineptitude, that gardening has become my delight. I too sense God's presence in my garden in ways I cannot explain. "To me the meanest flower that blows can give thoughts that do often lie too deep for tears."[9] Why this sentiment? What is this beauty I see?

"Beautiful things are those which please when seen," Aquinas said, but his answer has never quite satisfied me. It merely evokes another question: why are some things pleasing when seen? Explanations elude me. Beauty is intuitive, instinctive, I think, but inexplicable. I don't know what beauty *is*, but I know it when I see it, and I think you do too.

Beauty, however, as pleasing as it is, does not exist for itself. In fact, beauty for the sake of beauty diminishes beauty, as art for the sake of art diminishes art. We've all had the experience of seeing or possessing something exquisitely beautiful and finding sooner or later that it has lost its appeal. We no longer see it as a beautiful thing. Indeed, we no longer see it at all.

No, beauty looks *beyond* itself. It points to something richer and better; it "leads and lends to further sweetness, / Fuller, higher, deeper than its own."[10]

Philosopher and poet Samuel Coleridge made the same point in an essay in which he recalled the reaction of two tourists admiring a waterfall. One thought it was "pretty"; the other considered it "sublime"—so awe-inspiringly beautiful that it evoked reverence. Coleridge thought the latter sentiment preferable. When one sees authentic beauty, the only appropriate response is to kneel.

Lately, however, my eyes have been opened to a deeper beauty than I see in my garden. It's the loveliness of old friends whose goodness can only be described as beautiful. Where goodness flourishes so does beauty, and there's nothing quite so lovely as one whom God has made strong, radiant, and beautiful.[11] Folks like that make me long for the goodness that can produce such loveliness and for the One who is its source. It tells me how beautiful He must be who first thought of beauty and by His word brought it into being.

Early Greek writers understood this correlation between goodness and beauty and coined a word for it: *kalokagathon*, a contraction of three words—*kalos* (beautiful), *kai* (and) and *agathon* (good). *Kalokagathon* doesn't appear in the New Testament,[12] but was often used by early Christian writers. Ignatius, a first-century believer, wrote,

> None of these things escapes your notice, if you are maturing in faith and love towards Jesus Christ. For these are the beginning and end of life: faith is the beginning, and love is the end, and the two, when they exist in unity, are Godlike. Everything

· · · · · · · · · · · · · · · · · · ·

else that contributes to moral beauty (*kalokagath-ian*) follows from them.[13]

This notion of goodness as *moral* beauty intrigues me as I age, for *mortal* beauty is like a flower that, for all its loveliness, soon withers away. We're amazed, as we look in the mirror, how rapidly whatever portion of "good looks" we once enjoyed has faded away. The beauty of holiness, on the other hand, is "unfading."[14]

How can we have this amaranthine beauty? "Faith is the beginning," Ignatius said. Goodness and saintly character is the work of God, the product of humble dependence on Him. We must ask for it every day.

"The LORD takes pleasure in His people," Israel's psalmist said. "*He* will *beautify* the humble."[15]

MIXED UP IN MY HEAD

Just a line to say I'm living,
That I'm not among the dead,
Though I'm getting more forgetful
And mixed up in my head.

I got used to my arthritis
To my dentures I'm resigned.
I can manage my bifocals,
But my, I miss my mind!

—AUTHOR UNKNOWN

One of the hard facts of aging is the loss of mental acuity: I find now that my arguments are less compelling, my thoughts are less cogent, my memory is less clear. Little by little I'm losing my wits—a thought that disconcerts me, for as my physical abilities decline, all that remains is my mind.

I find encouragement, however, in the realization that the loss of my mental faculties, like everything else that I'm losing, can lead me to more of God, an idea George MacDonald elaborates in his *Diary of an Old Soul*:

> Well may this body poorer, feebler grow!
> It is undressing for its last sweet bed;
> But why should the soul, which death shall never
>   know,
> Authority, and power, and memory shed?
> It is so that love with absolute faith would wed;
> God takes the inmost garments off his child,
> To have him in his arms, naked and undefiled.

As we take leave of our senses we're left with God alone—which, after all, is His final intention for you and for me. His eternal aim is to bring us to the place where all that we have and all that we desire is *God*. There, and only there, will we find the satisfaction we've been seeking all our lives. As a friend of mine once put it: "I had no idea what I was missing until all I had left was God."

There's another truth that fills what's left of my mind with joy and thanksgiving, and it's the realization that the deepest knowledge of God is not the fruit of intelligence, but of obedience. Deep wisdom is the outgrowth of compliance: Those who "perfect holiness in the fear of God" have a degree of clarity and understanding that others do not have. John Calvin is often cited in this regard: "All knowledge of God is born of obedience."

In this world we *know* and then we do. But God turns our theory of knowledge upside down. In His world we *do* and then we know. Every act of obedience quickens our sensitivity to God. It awakens our sense of His presence and deepens our capacity to comprehend the truth He has given us to know. Even the *desire* to obey opens our eyes to see more of God than we could otherwise see. "If anyone *wills to do His will,* he shall know concerning the doctrine, whether it is from God or *whether* I speak on My own authority," Jesus said.[16]

The corollary to this principle is that those who are unwilling to do God's will have no knowledge of His ways. Blindness, error, and ignorance follow them throughout their lives. Ignorance and heresy, thus, are not a matter of the intellect, but of the heart. "They [the unbelieving] are darkened in their understanding and separated from the life of God because of the ignorance that is in them *due to the hardening of their hearts.*"[17]

Bad behavior blinds men and women to the truth so that they "believe the lie."[18] They perish because they refuse to love the truth and so be saved. They are deluded because they have "delighted in wickedness."[19] Heresy, then, is not a matter of confusion, but of morality. Heretics, Paul notes, are not merely self-deceived; they are "depraved."[20]

C. S. Lewis states the principle this way: "What you see and what you hear depends a good deal on where you are standing. It also depends on what sort of person you are."[21]

Put another way, it's the pure in heart who see God.[22]

> The soul's dark cottage, batter'd and decay'd,
> Lets in new light through chinks that Time has
>   made;
> Stronger by weakness, wiser, men become
> As they draw near their eternal home.
> —Edmund Waller (1606–1687)

My Staff

I'm growing fonder of my staff;
I'm growing dimmer in the eyes;
I'm growing fainter in my laugh;
I'm growing deeper in my sighs;
I'm growing careless of my dress;
I'm growing frugal of my gold;
I'm growing wise; I'm growing—yes—
I'm growing old.
                              —JOHN GODFREY SAXE

There's an antique rack in the entrance to our home in which we keep the canes and walking sticks of several generations of our family. My favorite is a slender staff with a gold-plated knob, engraved with the initials "DHR." It belonged to Carolyn's great-grandfather, whose name was Daniel Henry Rankin. Curiously, my initials are the same.

My study houses another stick collection: my father's peeled, apple-wood walking stick and an ancient, gnarled, blackthorn shillelagh among others.

Outside in a barrel in our garage there's an assortment of cross-country ski poles, wading wands, and trekking sticks I've gathered over the years. One of these days, I'll probably trade them all in for handrails and a walker.

I think of old Jacob, worshiping and "leaning on his staff."[23] Like Jacob, I too am crippled, broken-down, and ruined. I'll always need something or someone to lean on.

These days, when I set out on an enterprise that seems daunting for me at my age, I take this staff along with me: "The LORD will go before [me]."[24]

When I see my friends struggling with sin and guilt, I hold up this rod: May they "have power . . . to grasp how wide and long and high and deep is the love of Christ, and to know this love that surpasses knowledge."[25]

When there seems to be no time for reflection and quiet waiting and I think I must act *now,* I remember this stay: "Be still, and know that I am God."[26]

When I note that my legs and heart have grown weaker and I can no longer wade swift streams, climb steep trails, and surmount other difficulties, I strengthen my inner person with this thought: God will not cast me away when I am old; He will not forsake me when my strength is gone. My strength now is in "quietness and confidence."[27]

When I think of death and its certainty, I remember God's faithfulness throughout my years: He has supported me with His right hand; He has guided me with His counsel; and "afterward [he] will take me into glory."[28]

These truths and others are "the very staff of my age, my very prop."[29]

Old Jacob, weary and worn-out—once strong, but now humbled and utterly dependent on God—worshiped, leaning on the top of his staff. Like Jacob, I'm growing old and fond of my staff. I aim to keep it close at hand.

> Lord
> With a crooked stick for a cane
> I'm limping home.
> Mocked and maligned
> Stooped and stupid
> Soiled and shabby
> I limp toward You.
> —Ruth Harms Calkin

An afterthought...

I re-read John Bunyan's *The Pilgrim's Progress* the other day and came across this passage: "After this, Mr. Ready-to-halt called for his fellow-pilgrims, and told them, saying, I am sent for, and God shall surely visit you also. So he desired Mr. Valiant to make his will. And because he had nothing to bequeath to them that should survive him but his crutches, and his good wishes, therefore thus he said:

These crutches I bequeath to my son that shall tread in my steps, with a hundred warm wishes that he may prove better than I have been."[30]

My staffs and crutches I bequeath to our three sons.

IT'S ABOUT TIME

High notions of oneself are annihilated
by a glance in the mirror.
　　　　　—NOBEL POET, CZESLAW MILOSZ

A Botox cosmetic ad appears on our television screen every once in awhile that features a stunningly beautiful young model who smiles at her audience and murmurs, "It's about time." Exactly!

Time is the enemy. We invest in vitamin supplements, serums, tightening concentrates, firming creams, cellulite removers—a plethora of pills and potions—in an effort to stave off the effects of free-radical damage and try to live, or at least look alive, as long as possible. We battle every age spot, blemish, and bulge, but nothing works very well, or for very long. The hours fill our brow with lines and wrinkles, Shakespeare lamented. Time overwhelms us. We look our age, and it's not a pretty sight to see.

Which is exactly the point: time takes our "good looks" away. Jeremy Taylor, writing in the seventeenth century, put his finger on the issue. "First, age takes those parts that serve for ornamentation." Thus, "every day calls for a reparation of that portion which death fed on all night." Each morning we have to repair the damage that was done the night before. As an old friend of mine says: "A little powder, a little paint, makes a girl seem what she ain't."

And don't think for a minute that men are immune to this compulsion. We too are appalled by what we see in the mirror, and each morning must give ourselves to restoration. But no matter what, the trend is downward. It's about time.

We, however, are not about time. The God of all grace has called us to *eternal* glory![31] In the end, our bodies will be rescued from the tyranny of change and decay, and we will share in the glory that belongs to us as the children of God! When Christ is revealed, we will be revealed in everlasting splendor.[32] If we could but see ourselves today as we shall be *then*, we would be left speechless in awe and wonder. (I must add, however, that then, we'll not be self-conscious at all, but consumed with admiration for the beauty that we see in others.)

In the meantime, though the outward person is perishing, we can invest in inward loveliness. The more we center on inner beauty, the less preoccupied we'll be with that external glory that is inexorably fading away.

Here's the thing: What I hold in my mind will, in

time, show up in my face, for as George MacDonald once pointed out, the face is "the surface of the mind." If I cling to bitterness and resentment, if I tenaciously hold a grudge, if I fail to forgive, my countenance will begin to reflect those angry moods. My mother used to tell me that a mad look might someday freeze on my face. She was wiser than she knew.

But in the same way, a generous and charitable heart, one filled with grace and forgiveness, will find its way to the surface—for goodness cannot be hidden—and show itself in kind eyes and a face that is gentle and wise.

So my task is not to try to fix my face and make it good (that would be hypocrisy), but to set about killing the ugly things that come out of my heart—"so ugly that they make the very face over them ugly also" (George MacDonald).

Yet I know my heart—how hard it is, how disinclined to change. No one but God can drive its sullen self-centeredness away. So I must ask Him by His power to fulfill every desire for goodness. Then, someday, my face may reflect the holiness He has put into my heart.

I have a friend, a Catholic priest, who served as Mother Teresa's translator when she was here in the United States to address the United Nations. I was in his study one day and spied a picture of the two of them standing together on the streets of New York. I marveled again at her ancient, wrinkled, leathered, lined face, utterly unadorned. Wisdom had softened her face; character had drawn its lines. Gazing at those marks of courage and kindness, I thought: *Is there anyone more homely—or more beautiful?*

Hers was the beauty of holiness. May it be ours as well.

No Need for Regret

In the rash lustihead of my young powers,
I shook the pillaring hours,
And pulled my life upon me. Grimed with smears,
I stand amidst the dust o' the mounded years—
My mangled youth lies dead beneath the heap.
—FRANCIS THOMPSON, "THE HOUND OF HEAVEN"

Some folks try to romanticize youth, but I don't remember it that way. "Carefree youth" is an oxymoron to me.

My adolescence was a perfectly miserable time—years when I tore down family traditions and my inhibitions and prostituted the strength and vigor of youth on myself. I was an "angel-like spright with black sinne," John Donne would say, and lived with my fair share of guilt and self-reproach. Thus I pray with David, "Remember not the sins of my youth and my rebellious ways."[33]

"If only I could live my life over again," we say, "I would do better." Not likely. A fresh start for any of us would amount to almost nothing without the experience necessary to make the right adjustments. "The light which experience gives us is a lantern on the stern, which shines only on the waves behind us," Coleridge said. Lacking the knowledge and understanding we've gained through the years, we'd make the same mistakes again.

I came across a poem by poet Hezekiah Butterworth one day that frightened me a good deal:

I walked through the woodland meadows,
Where sweet the thrushes sing;
And I found on a bed of mosses
A bird with a broken wing.
I healed its wound, and each morning
It sang its old sweet strain;
But the bird with a broken pinion
Never soared as high again.

I found a young life broken
By sin's seductive art
And touched with a Christlike pity,
I took him to my heart.
He lived with a noble purpose,
And struggled not in vain;
But the life that sin had stricken
Never soared as high again.

I said to myself, "Is it true? Have my sins irreparably stricken and crippled me? Can I never soar as high again?"

Indeed we can—all of us—for God does *not* remember the sins of our youth. Love has paid the price, and thus our most outrageous and oft-repeated sins have been forgiven according to God's mercy and grace. We cannot drift beyond His love and care. Beyond the bad news of our failure is the good news of grace—the stupendous free gift of God.

Grace means that God forgives us, no matter what we have done, are doing, or will ever do again. It means that our sins are gone forever—replaced by Love.

Our Lord gives us this assurance: "Whoever comes to me I will *never* drive away."[34] He freely pardons; He abundantly forgives.[35] We will be welcomed, no matter what we have done, if only we will come to Him.

Grace also means that God has given us the resources to make a new beginning. The question is not, "Can I make it? Am I able? Can I overcome my habitual sin?" The question is, "Is *He* able?" Can *He* transform me?" He says He can, though it may take awhile. Love perfects that which it begins. He will not forsake the work of His hands.[36]

We must start with God's part, with the calm assurance that grace for the next act of obedience is already there. We don't have to worry about tomorrow, or this afternoon; we can move forward without fear or frustration knowing that the next step will take care of itself. That's the comfort we need to give to ourselves.

Furthermore, we must know that God's love will *continue* to cover our sins, no matter what we do. God is never disappointed—nor is He surprised—by human failure, for it is inevitable. "It is a consoling idea," wrote Danish philosopher Søren Kierkegaard, "that we are *always* in the wrong."

Long ago God made provision for our evil. Before we were born, before we did anything good or bad, Jesus paid for *all* our sins—those that were, those that are, and those that shall be. Now, despite false starts and failures, God is at work conforming some small part of us to His likeness, making us His portrait, His reproduction, His work of fine art. We can be confident of this: "He who began a good work in [us] will carry it on to completion."[37]

God is never in a hurry, but He does mean business. He will finish the work as soon as He can.

"But" we say, "I have wasted so much of my life. Can I still be of use?" God wastes nothing, not even our sins. When acknowledged, they humble us and make us more merciful to others in their weakness. We can become more approachable, more useful to God and to others. Indeed, each loss has its own compensation.

And there is more: Sin can make us more appreciative of God's forgiveness and can lead us to a deeper, more extravagant love for Him than we could otherwise attain. Once we know how much we've been forgiven, we love Him all the more.[38] Thus "broken pinions" heal fully and we can fly.

Another poet has amended Butterworth's lines:

The soul that comes to Jesus
    Is cleansed from every stain;
And by grace that is freely given,
    We *can* soar higher again.

IN THIS PLACE

Being born is the front end of our troubles.
—MISTER ROGERS

As a young man I was led to believe that the end of life would be easier than its beginning, but as I've aged I've come to the conclusion that some of the hardest tests are farther along.

Take Abraham, for example. After enduring a lifetime of difficulty, the old patriarch finally retired to a life of ease and affluence near the wells of Beersheba. He and Sarah enjoyed good old age with Isaac, their love and laughter. They were in their "golden years."

One night Abraham put his head on his pillow, thanked God for His goodness, and went to sleep, only to be jolted awake in the middle of the night by a voice beckoning him. "Abraham!"

"Here I am," Abraham replied.

"Take your son, your only son, Isaac, whom you love, and go to the region of Moriah. Sacrifice him there as a burnt offering on one of the mountains I will tell you about."[39]

Isaac was the son of Abraham's old age, the promised child through whom God pledged to make him great. Abraham knew that the gods of the Chaldeans and Canaanites demanded human sacrifice. Was his God now demanding this of him?[40] Why?

Indeed, we ask when life is sweet and then turns bitter, "Why?"

Did Abraham tell Sarah? I don't know. The ancient rabbis thought so, and said that Sarah held Isaac all that night, and that the ordeal contributed to her death.[41] But, for myself, I think Abraham told no one. This was a matter he had to work out with God alone.

Early the next morning Abraham packed up and started his terrible journey to Mount Moriah. There, the two—Abraham and his son—began their ascent to "the place" that God had revealed.[42]

Isaac turned to his father and spoke: "Father, the fire and wood are here, but where is the lamb for the burnt offering?" Abraham replied, "God himself will provide." With those words he rested his case.

You know the story: "Abraham looked up and there in a thicket he saw a ram caught by its horns. He . . . took the ram and sacrificed it as a burnt offering instead of his son."[43] Thus "Abraham called that place The LORD Will Provide," a saying that has been preserved to this day as a proverb and a promise: "On the mountain of the LORD it will be provided."

So, what of Abraham's stern "test"? What does it mean for me?

It comes to this: Can I endure the loss of anything I deem essential to life and believe that "in this place" of death and grief my God can and will provide?

I think of this as I stare in stark unbelief at what God is asking some of my friends to endure: critical illness, crippling infirmity, isolation and dislocation, the inability to use the talents and abilities with which they hoped to serve God to the end of their days. "Is this what He is asking of *me*?" my heart cries out.

Yet I know that there is love and logic in all God will ask of me. My losses—whatever they may be— are to the end that He may use me in a greater way to bring glory to His name and salvation to the world. Thus God swore to Abraham: "Because you have done this and have not withheld your son, your only son, I will surely bless you and make your descendants as numerous as the stars in the sky and as the sand on the seashore. Your descendants will take possession of the cities of their enemies, and through your offspring all nations on earth will be blessed, because you have obeyed me."

Now, God said to Abraham, the fruitfulness of your life will be manifest.

When you and I come to "the place" where we offer up all that we are and have to God—even the best gifts He has given us—*then* we will become a blessing to everyone we touch. This is the record of all whose lives have counted for God.

Is this not what Jesus meant when He promised, "Whoever loses his life for my sake will find it"?[44]

An afterthought ...

I cannot leave this story without mentioning that David purchased Moriah from Aravnah the Canaanite to mark the place where Abraham offered up Isaac. It was there that Solomon built the temple. Moriah is not a single peak, but an elongated ridge that begins at the junction of the Kidron and Hinnom Valleys and rises to its summit just northwest of the present Damascus Gate. There is sound archeological evidence to suppose that Jesus was crucified there on the summit, "on that place." And I fail to see how anyone reading about old Abraham, leading his dear son up the flanks of Mount Moriah, binding him to the altar while his heart breaks within him, can fail to miss the parallel with God leading His own Son to that same mountain centuries later "to the place of the Skull" (John 19:17). There He made the provision upon which all other provisions are based.

Did Abraham know? Perhaps this is what Jesus meant when He said, "Abraham rejoiced at the thought of seeing my day; he saw it *and was glad*" (John 8:56).

A LITTLE BIRD TOLD ME[45]

Said the robin to the sparrow,
"I would really like to know,
Why these anxious human beings,
Rush about and worry so?"

Said the sparrow to the robin,
"Oh, I think that it must be,
That they have no Heavenly Father,
Such as cares for you and me."

—UNKNOWN

The silence of our summer evening was broken by the loud, persistent, and frantic "Tweet! Tweet! Tweet!" of the mother robin. Not just any robin, mind you. This is *our* Robin, with four newly hatched young in her well-tended nest, which she has carefully crafted and anchored securely in one of the tall junipers against our back fence.

As she sounded the alarm, Papa and I both popped up and hustled outside in our sleep togs to see what had so ruffled Robin's feathers. Sure enough, we had an intruder. Through the gathering darkness, in the far corner of our backyard, we could see the threatening shape. There she crouched: The Cat!

Robin went on one dive-bombing mission after another, swooping as close to the enemy as she dared and loudly scolding with each attack. But to no avail. This tried and tested method, which worked with lesser foes like the squirrels, was useless now. Cat stood her ground, seeming to be seeking the right moment to advance on the weak and vulnerable baby birds.

Then out of the night came Papa, wildly waving his arms, lurching and leaping forward like something out of *Jurassic Park* and bellowing, "Scat! Shoo! Get out of here!"

Cat held her position as long as she could. Then realizing the new troops were too much for her, she did the smart thing and hastily retreated back over the fence into the safety of her own yard.

With all the precious treasure of the nest secure once again, Robin calmed down and peace returned to our neighborhood. And just before I drifted off to sleep I wondered about what Robin might be thinking of the whole affair.

If Robin could talk, how would she relate what happened? Would she even be aware of where help had really come from? Did she know that Someone powerful who cared for her and her concerns had heard her cries for help and had rushed to her aid?

The next morning at the birdbath would she say something like this to the birds of her feather as they flocked together: "Boy, I really had a scare last night. It was getting dark, and I made one last trip out to dig worms for the little ones. Just as I flew back toward home I noticed something was not right. Then I saw it. A big furry creature sneaking steadily toward my babies. Disaster on the move. Oh, I could see it coming!

"With my heart in my throat I knew I had to do something. Everything depended on me. I remembered all the articles I had read on assertiveness training and self-defense. I remembered reading *The Little Engine That Could.* I was terrified, but I reached way down inside myself to pull up the right stuff and started to go at that creature. I tried to intimidate the thing with loud, shrill sounds as I flew and fluttered in as close as I dared, then circled and flew back for another attack. For a while I was losing ground and the creature kept on coming. I was frantic and weak, but I kept up my harangue. And then the strangest thing happened. Suddenly, the creature turned and jumped away in the other direction. It took me a minute to calm down and realize that the danger was gone. I guess I really am something and have what it takes to take care of any situation. I noticed my People standing near the corner of their house. I guess they were pretty impressed with me too."

Or would Robin greet her friends in the morning with a tale like this: "Boy, I really had a scare last night. It was getting dark, and I made one last trip out to dig worms for the little ones. Just as I flew back toward home I noticed something was not right. Then I saw it. A big furry creature sneaking steadily toward my babies. Disaster on the move. Oh, I could see it coming!

"With my heart in my throat I knew I had to do something. I tried to intimidate the thing with loud, shrill sounds as I flew and fluttered in as close as I dared, then circled and flew back for another attack. But I could see I was losing ground. I was no match for this enemy. Then I remembered Someone who owned the bush where I had my nest. I knew He had smiled at me and was delighted with my new family. I knew He was big—much bigger than the creature named Disaster. So I did the right thing. I cried for help. And do you know what? He answered my cry and He rushed to help me. He knew just what to do and how best to protect me. I am really glad I recognized I needed help and called. Now I know even more that He cares for me and is there for me. He doesn't expect me to always know what to do and to always be strong. I want to remember to give credit where credit is due and to say, 'Thanks. I needed that!' Last night I had a big scare but I also learned a big lesson."

Dear Grands,

This little bird taught *me* a big lesson too. From her I learned to call out for help to my Heavenly Father when I feel weak and am facing something big and scary. I hope you will each do the same. Our God will come rushing to help because He delights in you even more than Papa delights in Robin.

With lots of love,
Nana

P. S. Have Mom or Dad read you Psalm 18:1–19 to see how this worked for someone else a long time ago.

BIRD SONG

Field and forest, vale and mountain,
Flow'ry meadow, flashing sea,
Chanting bird and flowing fountain
Call us to rejoice in Thee.
—GENEVAN PSALTER

Speaking of birds—Solomon describes old age as a time "when men rise up at the sound of birds, but all their songs grow faint."[46] He was right, of course, on both counts: I get up with the birds, but until I get my bearings and my hearing aid in place, I can't hear their songs. Thanks to the marvel of modern gadgetry, however, I *can* hear birds quite well these days, and their singing makes my heart swell with joy.

I read the other day that birds sing "because they can and because they must. Songs are used to attract mates and defend territories, but the form is much more than function. Nature is full of beauty, and of music." So writes David Rothenberg, a professor at New Jersey Institute of Technology.

The professor goes on to explain that birds sing because they have a syrinx instead of a larynx. The syrinx is a unique musical instrument that looks like a hollow, inverted Y that lies deep in a bird's chest at the point where the trachea divides into the two bronchia which rise from the lungs. Each leg of the Y rests on a separate bronchial tube, thus giving birds unusual control and creativity in the sounds they can make.

Birds can sing two different notes at the same time, or sing a duet with themselves. They are capable of singing a rising note with one side of the syrinx and a falling note with the other. They can use one side for low notes and the other for high ones, or switch from one side to the other in mid-note. No other creature is quite so versatile.

But what I ask is, *why* do birds sing—really? Why these tiny virtuosos? Why does "the air tremble with the din of songs and the whir of wings"?

Birds were brought into being before us to fill the earth with joyful music—to draw our hearts up to God in thanksgiving and adoration. Birds are "heaven's high and holy muses," John Donne said, daily reminders that God has given *us* a song so we may sing with them in praise and thanksgiving to our creator.

We can sing along with Israel's sweet singer:

"I will sing of your strength,
    in the morning I will sing of your love;

for you are my fortress,
> my refuge in times of trouble."[47]

We can "sing of the ways of the LORD, for the glory of the LORD is great."[48] We can "sing . . . for [the LORD] has done marvelous things; his right hand and his holy arm have worked salvation for [us]."[49] Or we can make up our very own song!

So, when you hear God's little hymn-birds break into carefree song each morning, echo their melodies with your own. Lift up your voice—harmonious, hoarse, or harsh—and join them in praise to your Creator, Redeemer, and Lord. Sing from your soul-nest.

But, you say, "I don't feel like singing this morning." All is still—no flutter, no melody? Sing anyway. There is grace sufficient to sing, and joy may surprise you as you make melody in your heart to the Lord. Give it a try. What do you have to lose but your sorrow?

Israel's poet observed:

"The birds of the air nest by the waters;
> they sing among the branches . . .
[Therefore] I will sing to the LORD all my life;
> I will sing praise to my God as long as I live."[50]

Counting the Days

*That flesh is but the [hour] glasse, which holds
   the dust
That measures all our time.*
—GEORGE HERBERT

Psalm 90 is "A Prayer of Moses," the wistful reflections and petitions of an old man. Here Moses, as Flannery O'Connor once pointed out, is in the most significant position life offers us: He is facing death.

Moses begins by pondering the vast difference between God and His creatures. He is eternal; we are not. He is "from everlasting to everlasting." We are ephemeral, swept away "in the sleep of death." We spring up like grass in the morning and by evening we are withered and dry, a little mound of dust.

"Why do we have to die?" I ask myself. God has put eternity in our hearts; we were made for immortality! Why does death sweep us away?

The answer comes as a complete surprise: Death is not our lot; it is our sentence. We are "consumed by

[God's] anger." We are mortal because we are sinful. "The wages of sin is death."[51]

To use Moses' words, we are "hurried away"[52] by God's indignation, which is why, I suppose, we keep looking at our watches. The "span" of our days passes quickly: *tempus fugit* (time flies), we say. No, "*we* fly away."[53] As the old hymn puts it:

Time, like an ever-rolling stream,
    Bears all its sons away;
They fly forgotten as a dream
    Dies at the op'ning day.[54]

So, I say to myself, it's a good thing to ponder the brevity of life now and then, and to number my days, as Moses suggests. Three-score and ten years are allotted, or four-score if I'm unduly strong. But in the end the grave gets us all.

I have to say, we don't think much about dying these days. In earlier times folks were more comfortable with the idea. Churches were surrounded by cemeteries and filled with sepulchers—somber reminders that one's body would one day lie under a slab. The village parson, George Herbert, said he frequented graveyards to "take acquaintance of this heap of dust."[55] Today, we want cemeteries to be out of town or out of sight, out of mind, as far away as possible.

So, what will take away our fear of death? It is

a promise of a "morning" that rends the skies, when we rise from "the sleep of death" that has swept us away.[56] This is the promise of the resurrection—a prospect that is a spring of invincible joy, a current of mirth under all our troubles. We can, as Moses insists, "be glad *all* our days."

So for the rest of our days on earth, we pray with Moses: "May the favor of the Lord our God rest upon us; establish [make permanent] the work of our hands for us." And may God direct us to do those things that have eternal significance: prayer, love, purity, wisdom, and quiet proclamation.

We pass through this world and on, like a swallow through a loft, but our influence can be eternal. We may not live long, but we can "live deep," as a friend of mine says. Then, when I have served God's purposes in my generation, I can fly away.[57]

There was a needlepoint plaque that hung on a wall in the home in which I grew up. (Thank you, Mother.) It meant very little to me then; it means a good deal to me now:

Only one life, 'twill soon be past;
Only what's done for Christ will last.
And when I am dying, how glad I will be,
That the lamp of my life has blazed out for Thee.

SAUNTERING

I am old and move slowly.
—SOCRATES

When I was a much younger man I used to run several miles a day. When my knees gave out I began to walk—first aerobically and then briskly. Now I saunter.

Henry David Thoreau, in an essay on walking, explains the origins of the word "saunter." He says the term comes from the Middle Ages, when wandering pilgrims would beg for alms to finance their journey to "*la Saint Terre*" (the Holy Land). Such people became known as "saint-terrers," or "saunterers."

I can't vouch for the etymology of the word, and I understand Thoreau's theory is in doubt these days, but I like his explanation better than any I've heard, for I myself am a saunterer, a wandering pilgrim, begging for grace, slowly making my way to the City of God.

Let's hear it for sauntering! My dictionary defines

the word as "to wander or walk about idly and in a leisurely or lazy manner; to lounge; to stroll; to loiter." That's me: God's loiterer, in no particular hurry, taking time to see the world around me and sample it along the way.

Very few people saunter these days. Most folks on the green belt here in Boise (where I saunter) are in a hurry—speed-walking, or racing around on mountain bikes, rollerblades, and skateboards. I wonder where they're going, or, as an old song by Alabama, the country group, suggests: "I'm in a Hurry (and Don't Know Why)."

The same can be said for God's people. So many of us seem to be in a hurry to get somewhere, running off to this meeting or that, signing up for one course or another, frantically working out our own salvation, sanctification, and service for God as though everything depends on us. I wish we all knew how to saunter.

It's a great art to saunter. And it grows out of the conviction that "all things are of God."[58] Oh, we must pursue God and His will for us with all our heart, but it is rest and peace to know that every aspect of our pilgrimage is in God's hands. He has freed us from past sin and guilt and is presently freeing us from its power. Our destiny is not riding on anything we do or have done or fail to do here on earth. It rests on the work of One who is faithful to the end.

So, "just go for walks" says Thomas Merton, "live

in peace, let change come quietly and invisibly on the inside."[59]

I find Merton's words bracing. Since God is at work in me and has promised that He will never forsake the work of His hands, I can trust Him to bring completion to the process He has begun. It's been my experience that whatever change takes place in me is fairly slow, occurring in some secret, hidden part of me and often imperceptible except in retrospect. There are even times of failure when I seem to be making no progress at all. I may even revert to old habits of behavior for a season—regressions that make me believe I've slipped back into old patterns of sin. It is good to remind myself in those times that it may be years later that I see what God has been doing. His pace, though inexorably steady and impossible to stop, is also excruciatingly slow.

In the meantime, while I saunter toward heaven and home, I can begin to pay attention to those who are in pilgrimage with me. I can take every occasion to listen, to love, and to pray, knowing that I don't have to rush about and make things happen. God himself has prepared good works for me to do.[60]

Thoreau was not a Christian, as far as I know, but he often wrote with luminous insight. Thus he concludes his essay on sauntering: "So we saunter toward the Holy Land; till one day the sun shall shine more brightly than ever he has done, shall shine into our minds and hearts, and light up our whole lives with a great awakening light, so warm and serene and golden as on a bank-side in autumn."

Thoreau was a wise man—wiser than he knew. Someday soon our "sun of righteousness will rise with healing in its wings"[61] and we shall settle into a *perfect* pace.

DANGEROUS CROSSINGS

Life is mighty chancy at any kind of trade.
—RUDYARD KIPLING

I don't wade swift streams any more, even when the best fishing lies on the other side of the river. The rocks are too slippery, the currents are too strong, my balance is too uncertain, and my old legs aren't what they used to be.

I take this as a parable for my life: So many challenges I once took on readily are now too challenging for me. Like the psalmist, I lose sleep at night wondering how I can negotiate them.[62]

But then I remember the deeds of the Lord. He led His "people like a flock." Like a good shepherd He brought all Israel safely through the Red Sea to the other side. His "path led through the sea, [His] way through the mighty waters."[63] No one was left behind, no one was abandoned, no one was swept away. God surged through the Red Sea as I would wade a tiny brook.

All of us face difficult and dangerous crossings in our lifetime—a transition to a new place or position, a decision to abandon a sinful practice and make a new beginning, a choice to walk a way we would rather not go, a call to venture ourselves in untried service, a retirement that takes us from prominence to a lower profile, or our final crossing through the river "bitter and cold." Yet we need not fear the dark currents, for God does not fear them. His strength and courage are infinite. He will see us through.

The psalmist observes, with some wonderment, that God leaves no footprints as He accompanies us. Just as the sand in the bottom of a stream hides our footprints as soon as they are imprinted, so God's presence, as real as our own, is hidden from us. He is with us, "walking incognito," as C. S. Lewis said, and thus we may not realize He is present. But, Lewis continues, "the incognito is not hard to penetrate. The real labor is to remember, to attend. In fact, to come awake. Still more, to remain awake,"[64] to make ourselves think about His presence, to remind ourselves that He is at our side.

Furthermore, though we cannot see God's footprints in our crossings, He is incarnate in human agents that we can see. At the Red Sea He led Israel "by the hand of Moses and Aaron." Think back to how He has led you—in the wise counsel of a mother, in the strong grip of a father, in the urgings of godly brother or sister, in the quiet encouragement of a caring spouse, in the gentle touch of a child.

How many hands have reached out to us—guiding us, encouraging us, strengthening us? In them we perceive the hand of our Lord leading us through deep and dangerous waters to the other side.

Hard crossings are inevitable, but our Lord has promised: "When you pass through the waters, I will be with you; and when you pass through the rivers, they will not sweep over you."[65]

> I came to the swift, raging river,
> And the roar held the echo of fear;
> "Oh, Lord, give me wings to fly over,
> If You are, as You promised, quite near."
> But He said, "Trust the grace I am giving,
> All-pervasive, sufficient for you.
> Take My hand—we will face it together,
> But My plan is not over but *through*."

—Lee Webber

DEFORMED

O God, I am too ugly for human beings, perhaps
you have a use for me.

—ST. VINCENT DE PAUL

I came across a tortured, twisted pine tree some years ago, high on a ridge overlooking Boulder Meadow—an ugly, misshapen thing at first glance. But I looked again and saw something deeper and better and thought of those whose deformities are overwhelmed by beauty.

Appearance is overrated, a mere sensation in the eyes (or brain) produced by shape, color, and motion and conditioned a good deal by society and association. (In some cultures, foot-long earlobes are considered the essence of loveliness.)

There is a spiritual beauty, however, that is much deeper and more enduring than anything we can see with our natural eyes. It is a symmetry and splendor that God brings to His children— the "beauty of holiness."

Our present culture turns the phrase upside down, worshiping instead the outward appearance—the holiness of beauty.[66] That's a terrible mistake, for it leads us to vanity—the desire to exceed the limits God has appointed for us—and is the means by which pride and self-preoccupation enter in and whereby we miss the highest good.

We must be satisfied with the way God has formed us. Our disabilities and deformities are not a mistake, but part of God's eternal plan. His way of dealing with them is not to remove them, but to endow them with godlike strength, dignity, and beauty and put them to His intended use.

McGuffey had it exactly right . . .

Beautiful faces are they that wear,
The light of a pleasant spirit there;
Beautiful hands are they that do,
Deeds that are noble, good and true;
Beautiful feet are they that go,
Swiftly to lighten another's woe.

—*McGuffey's Second Reader*

Has aging brought humiliating disfigurement? Do you consider yourself an eyesore, too ugly to be of use?

Do not believe that for a moment. No, you are "God's workmanship, created in Christ Jesus to do good works, which God prepared in advance for [you] to do."[67] You are His special creation, designed from birth to manifest God's loveliness in a unique way. The Craftsman's plan surpasses the material.

Your countenance, though wrinkled or blemished, can be adorned with the joy of the Lord and made lovely with His kindness and compassion. Your body, be it ever so humble and lumpish, can be graceful in unselfish service and love. This is "grace beyond reach of art," human ugliness hidden in divine loveliness, beauty at its best.

And, of course, this is not all that will be. On ahead lies the redemption of our bodies. We will be made new: "We are as God has made us, but we are not as God *will* make us. We will be made over again and everything will once for all be set right" (George MacDonald).

And so I pray, may the beauty of the Lord our God be upon *you*.

Odd, this twisted form
    should be the work of God.
God, who makes, without mistakes,
    the happy norm, the status quo—
the usual—made me, you know.

The Royal Palm He made;
    and, too, the stunted pine.

With joy I see the lovely shapes;
    with pride I live in mine.
No accident I am:
    a Master Craftsman's plan.

—Ruth Bell Graham

DRESSED FOR SUCCESS

*The wearer of Grandmother's (Wisdom's) clothes
never thinks about how he or she looks, but thinks
how handsome other people are.*
—GEORGE MACDONALD, *THE GOLDEN KEY*

I recently came across Washington Irving's description of a friend with whom he fished one of the tributaries of the Hudson River:

One of our party had equaled the Don [Quixote] in the fullness of his equipments, being attired capa-pie [from head to foot] for the enterprise. He wore a broad-skirted fustian [pretentious] coat, perplexed with half a hundred pockets; a pair of stout shoes and leathern gaiters; a basket slung on one side for fish; a patent rod, a landing net, and a score of other inconveniences only to be found in the true angler's armory. Thus harnessed for the field, he was as great a matter of stare and wonderment among the country folk, who had never

seen a regular angler, as was the steel-clad hero
of La Mancha among the goatherds of the Sierra
Morena.[68]

Nothing has changed. Anglers still hope to be
properly "harnessed" for the field, and, truth be told,
to become the objects of the stares and wonderment
of those that see them on-stream. The only difference
between Irving's day and ours is that our equipment
has become more sophisticated, and Orvis, Winston,
Sage, and Simms have put their brands on our "armory." It's a matter of looking good.

That goes for our street clothes as well, except they
bear other brand names such as L.L.Bean and REI—
at least for me. One purpose of clothing, I suppose, is
to cover up our less-presentable parts, as Paul would
say, as our parts grow less presentable each year.

It seems to me, though, that no matter what
we wear, we ought to dress down rather than up.
Advertisements entice us to be noticed, but God's men
and women have a different motivation: we should be
"clothed with humility," one practical application of
which is the desire to blend in and not attract attention to ourselves.

This generally means that we dress convention-
ally, the way most people would dress on a given occasion. Being flamboyant can draw attention to us,
but so can being frumpy or out of fashion. Augustine
taught his students, "Do not attract attention by the

way you dress. Endeavor to impress by your manner of life, not by the clothes you wear." I think that's good counsel for all ages.

One practical result of getting this idea into our hearts is that we become less preoccupied with how *we* look and can "think more highly of others than we think of ourselves."

Clothing is a necessity mandated by the Fall and our subsequent self-consciousness. But maintaining a wardrobe can be a tedious process, which gets more tiresome as we age, particularly as we get less interested in impressing others. Then the thought occurred to me one morning, after I read Jeremy Taylor's advice in his diary, that I could make the morning ritual of dressing myself more meaningful if I view it as a reminder of the spiritual apparel with which I'm clothed.

> In your dressing, let there be ejaculations fitted to the several actions of dressing: as at washing your hands and face, pray God to cleanse your Soul from sin; in putting on your clothes, pray him to clothe your Soul with the righteousness of your Savior; and so in all the rest. For Religion must not only be the garment of your Soul, to invest it all over; but it must be also as the fringes to every of your actions, that something of Religion appear in every one of them, besides the innocence of all of them.[69]

What Taylor is suggesting is that we use each item of clothing to remind ourselves of our spiritual vestments. It's a contrivance I've been using for a while now.

When I put on my shirt each morning, I remind myself to "put on love." Perhaps I can do nothing more than love someone today, but it's enough. Love is the best gift I can give to God and to others throughout the day.

When I buckle my trousers, I'm reminded that I need to "gird up the loins" of my mind—pull my thoughts together and fix my hope fully on the gift of eternal life that will be brought to me when I see my Savior face to face. That's a thought that brings sobriety and peace.

When I lace up my boots, I think of my feet as shod and prepared to go wherever God wants me to go today and to go the distance—whatever it may be—to bring the good news of reconciliation and peace to others.

When I strap on my watch, I think of the need to redeem the time—to use each hour to be a benediction to others. "Evil days are days of opportunity," I say to myself. Many that I meet today have been ravaged by evil and are living in terrible sorrow. "May I be a blessing to them," I pray.

When I pick up my hat, I'm reminded of our ultimate and certain salvation—a salvation that is promised and secure. I am the apple of God's eye, as dear as God's only-begotten Son.

Silly, you say? Works for me. It's a great way to dress for success.

Is This All the Thanks I Get?

*Teach me, Lord, not to gather encouragement
from appreciation by others, lest this should interfere with purity of motive—not to seek praise,
respect, gratitude, or regard from superiors or
equals on account of age, or past service.*

—EDWARD BENSON FROM *PRAYERS,*
PUBLIC AND PRIVATE

For several years Carolyn and I, somewhat like Job, sat in a "Nash heap"—a 1959, porcelain-white Nash Rambler station wagon that looked for all the world like an inverted bathtub on wheels. If it were turned upside down, I could have clamped an outboard motor on the rear bumper and raced the thing in Vancouver's annual Nanaimo Bathtub Regatta.

I still remember the day we began visiting car lots to replace it. We looked at a number of shiny new vehicles and finally decided on a purchase. Unfortunately, the payments were more than we could carry.

We dickered for a while with the salesman—his

price and ours—but concluded that the twain would never meet and hastened to make our departure. As we were leaving his office, the salesman gave us his best shot. "Hey, you guys deserve this car," he shouted. In my heart of hearts I responded, "Indeed we do!"

Entitlement has always been one of my soft spots. "I've been a pretty good guy," I say to myself. "My accomplishments deserve a bit of praise." Which is why I get my nose out of joint when people don't appreciate me.

Then one day I came upon God's word to Zechariah about a shepherd who dedicated himself to the good of his people, who encouraged peace, prosperity, and brought tranquility and harmony to his flock. He, however, far from being appreciated, was despised and rejected. Those who discarded him set his price at thirty pieces of silver, the value of a slave.[70] Should I expect more?

And then there is Solomon's tale of "a small city with only a few people in it, and a powerful king who . . . surrounded it and built huge siege works against it." But, "there lived in that city a man poor but wise, and he saved the city by his wisdom." Let's hear it for the wise man! What will he receive for his efforts? Alas, "nobody remembered that poor man."[71]

One of the things I'm learning as I grow older is not to expect too much from people. It's possible to pour a good deal of effort, energy, and love into a friend or family member and receive nothing but ingratitude for our efforts. It's even possible that others may receive credit for the good that we've done.

We should all express appreciation to those who come to our side, but if we expect everyone to recognize what we have done for them, we can be deeply hurt. And we'll soon be asking ourselves: "Is this all the thanks I get?"

It's good, in those times of disappointment, to look into our own motives: Do we have an unholy sense of entitlement, or a passion to be seen and applauded for our efforts? Can we give freely and allow others to take responsibility for their own responses?

There are grateful men and women in this world, and we may hear from them. But the statistics in Jesus' parable of the ten virgins suggest that perhaps only ten percent of those we love and serve will ever thank us. The others will be silent at best. At worst they may be hostile.[72] So if even one has responded, be grateful. And remember—God *alone* enables us to do good things for others.

> And if the love of a grateful heart
> As a rich reward be given,
> Lift thou the love of a grateful heart
> To the God of Love in Heaven."[73]

Ingratitude in others can embitter us if we're not watchful. We must forgive those who fail to thank us—even those who, despite the love we've bestowed upon them, have turned away from us. Jesus said, "Love your enemies, do good to them, and lend to them *without expecting to get anything back*. Then your reward will be great, and you will be sons of the Most High, because he is kind to the *ungrateful . . .*"[74]

Our Lord will be "kind" to *us* when we see Him face to face, for we too have been ungrateful. His "well-done" will ring throughout the universe, and He will praise us before human beings and angels. This may be the only appreciation we receive for the good we've done on earth, but in the end it's the only praise that will matter.

And though we cannot do much about those who disregard us, we can do a good deal about ourselves. Sometimes in the busyness of our lives we fail to express the appreciation to those who have contributed so much to us—parents, spouses, siblings, friends, teachers, mentors, colleagues, to name only a few. Yet it doesn't take much time or effort to express our gratitude—a brief but heartfelt word of appreciation, a phone call, a text message, an e-mail, or a thank-you note will do.

Speaking of which, Carolyn and I have often marveled at our culture's indifference to thank-you notes. "I don't write little thank-you notes," a man said recently in our hearing. We could only stare in amazement. Is this refinement and courtesy so frivolous that it's now beneath us?

"Sending thank-you notes has become a lost art," mourns Mary Mitchell, a syndicated columnist who writes under the name of *Ms. Demeanor.* "A grateful attitude is a tremendous life skill, and an efficient and inexpensive way to set ourselves apart in the work force and in our adult lives . . . The habit of manners comes from inside—it's an attitude based on respecting other people."

Appreciation is an attitude based on respect for other people, even the unkind and ungrateful. But primarily it is an attitude based on love, for "love has good manners."[75] And the habit of thankfulness must come from inside, for gratitude is the work of God's Holy Spirit. Apart from His grace, we would all be ungrateful wretches.

"Mine Eyes Have Seen the Glory"

O! but we shall keep
Our vision still. One moment was enough,
We know we are not made of mortal stuff.
And we can bear all trials that come after:
The hate of men and the fool's loud bestial
    laughter;
And Nature's rule and cruelties unclean
For we have seen the Glory—we have seen.

—C. S. LEWIS FROM *SPIRITS IN BONDAGE:*
A CYCLE OF LYRICS, "DUNGEON GRATES"

We think of youth as the prime of life, when we have our wits about us. But, as Shakespeare's Dogberry lamented, "When the age is in, the wit is out. God help us!"[76]

Psychologist B. F. Skinner said, "It is easier to be happy when you're young . . . old age is not the 'best part.'" But Skinner was a behaviorist, who saw human activity as little more than conditioned response. Furthermore, his model was unredeemed humanity. The apostle Paul had the true and much better perspective.

> Therefore we do not lose heart. Though outwardly we are wasting away, yet inwardly we are being renewed day by day. For our light and momentary troubles are achieving for us an eternal glory that far outweighs them all. So we fix our eyes not on what is seen, but on what is unseen. For what is seen is temporary, but what is unseen is eternal (2 Corinthians 4:16–18).

Gerontologists tell us we're three ages at once: chronological, physiological, and psychological. Our chronological age is a function of our years. Our physiological age is a measure of our physical well-being. Our psychological age is the age that we "feel." And I would add a fourth: our spiritual age. This is the true measure of our maturity. It's not a date on our calendar; it's a state of mind.

Age has its troubles—diminished hearing and eyesight, forgetfulness, aching backs and arthritic hands, sleepless nights, faltering steps, crippled knees. These are what Paul calls light, momentary troubles—incremental intimations that "we are wasting away." Yet Paul insists that "*inwardly* we are being renewed day by day," for our present, temporal troubles are at work to produce an *eternal* weight of glory.[77]

How so?

Well, as I see it, aging and weakness send our thoughts after God. We learn to "fix our eyes" on Him and on unseen realities; we gain insight to distinguish between the temporary and the timeless, the permanent and the passing. We are drawn by God's love; we set our affections on things above and not on things on the earth.

Here is a state of mind, I say, a way of looking at things: It is a matter of seeing what cannot be seen with natural eyes: *envisioning the eternal glory that awaits us.* It is looking beyond present frailty to what we will someday be—glorious creatures, bursting with radiant beauty and infinite energy!

So, with this vision, "We do not lose heart."[78] We can know strength of character despite our frail and failing humanity. We can show patient endurance and love for others in the midst of our discomfort. We can partner with our pain and go on serving, praying, loving, and caring to the end of our days. We can be joyful and confident at the edge of death. *We can press on, because we have seen the glory!*

We're all growing older and feeling more of the effects of aging every day. This is "Nature's rule and cruelties unclean." The question is this: How do we view our troubles? Are they driving us toward bitterness and despair? Or are they drawing us into deeper intimacy with God?

If we are growing toward Him, we will see more of

the glory than ever before, for that assurance comes
not from texts or creeds, but from daily communion
with the God of life who loves us as no one else can.
Thus, Isaiah encourages us:

> "Arise, shine, for your light has come,
>   and the glory of the LORD rises upon you."[79]

THE GRANDER CURVES OF CHARACTER

Dear Pastor,
I know God loves everybody, but I don't think he
ever met my sister.
Yours sincerely,

ARNOLD, AGE 8

It's not easy to endure, let alone love someone who makes your life miserable, which is why David's poem in praise of Saul is so laudable:

Saul and Jonathan—
> in life they were loved and gracious,
> and in death they were not parted.
They were swifter than eagles,
> they were stronger than lions.
O daughters of Israel,
> weep for Saul,
> who clothed you in scarlet and finery,
> who adorned your garments with ornaments
> of gold.[80]

"Saul and Jonathan—in life they were loved and gracious." What a remarkable thing to say!

David had good reason, of course, to eulogize his dear friend Jonathan, every memory of whom was a benediction, but Saul was another matter entirely. Saul's resentment and insane rage had driven him to harass David unmercifully. He had hounded David for years, pursuing him like "a partridge in the mountains."[81] Yet David crowds what praise he can utter of Saul into these lines.

In doing this, however, David did not lie. There were things he could not say of Saul. But he did commend what he knew was good and true about the man: his courage, his military skill, his willingness to aid those in need, his pleasantness and courtesy when he was in his right mind. David resisted the temptation to dwell on Saul's vices and chose instead to reflect on his virtues.

And so I've been asking myself lately: Am I preoccupied with other people's imperfections? Do I brood over their failures and faults, their moral flaws? Do I consider only the wrong that they do, especially the wrong they have done to me, or do I reflect on those aspects of character that are morally excellent and worthy of praise?

How many friendships have ended because someone's mistakes loomed large in our minds? How many marriages have died because we brooded and obsessed over our spouse's flaws? How many of us have alienated our children because we have endlessly chided them and harped on their failings?

Paul writes, "Whatever is true, whatever is noble, whatever is right, whatever is pure, whatever is lovely, whatever is admirable—if anything is excellent or praiseworthy—think about such things."[82] I've often pondered this verse and wondered how anyone can think abstractly about nobility, righteousness, and loveliness. Can it be that Paul is suggesting that we concentrate on those traits in others that are noble, admirable, lovely, and worthy of praise?

Love is not gullible or naïve, but when we "love each other deeply . . . love covers over a multitude of sins."[83] Love looks for goodness and nobility in others. When we do this, we gain perspective and admiration for the merits of friends, family, neighbors, and colleagues despite their flaws.

> So in the survey of his worth the small
> Asperities of his spirit disappear,
> Lost in the grander curves of character.[84]

"Love one another and you will be happy," Michael Leunig writes. "It's as simple and as difficult as that."[85]

Philosopher Peter Kreeft says that "our loving can be like a tube open at both ends, with God's love coming in one end and out the other . . . The alternative is to be a tube open at only one end. Then we try to squeeze our own toothpaste out of the tube. But we have only a finite amount of spiritual toothpaste to give. So we worry about squandering it, just as the older brother in the parable of the prodigal son did. But God's supply is infinite."[86]

God's love flowing in from one end of the tube to the other floods all our being so that we can pour out our love to others. But we can only love because we know that God first loved us."

"We must lie where John did, on the bosom of incarnate Love, until we begin to love as He."[87]

O Love that will not let me go,
I rest my weary soul in thee;
I give thee back the life I owe,
That in thine ocean depths its flow
May richer, fuller be.[88]

GOING AND NOT KNOWING

*God of the coming years, through paths unknown
we follow Thee.*

—HUGH T. KERR[89]

Abraham was seventy-five years of age when he was taken from his home in Ur of the Chaldees. His entire life from that time on became nomadic as he moved from one place to another—from Ur to Haran, to Shechem, to Bethel, to Egypt, to the Negev, to Hebron . . . "By faith Abraham . . . obeyed and went, even though he did not know where he was going."[90] Rootless, homeless, going and not knowing—that was the story of his life.

In thinking about Abraham's changing environment, it occurred to me that aging itself is a journey away from settled and secure places to endless change, uncertainty, and adjustment. It is transition from a familiar past to an uncertain future. It is movement from a family home, to a smaller place, to a daughter's home, to a retirement community, to a nursing home—the "last resort," as a friend of mine says. Sociologist Paul Tournier describes the experience as always being "in between," like a trapeze artist suspended in mid-air.

So, like Abraham, as we grow older we pass "through paths unknown," making our way from one place to another, always traveling, going and not knowing, "just lookin' for a home."[91] Yet we can be at home in every place we dwell, for our safekeeping lies not in the place, but in God himself. He is our home and our habitation. We dwell in the shelter of the Most High. We rest in the shadow of the Almighty.[92]

It is noteworthy that Abraham raised a rough-hewn altar in every place he lived. There, we're told, he "called on the name of the Lord"—he bowed his heart in worship.

Worship is the way we get our minds off our circumstances and ourselves and give our full attention to God. There, in His presence, under His wings, we find refuge. The eternal God becomes our dwelling place.[93]

Peter was told, "When you are old you will stretch out your hands, and someone else will dress you and lead you where you do not want to go." Nevertheless, Jesus called to him, "Follow me!"[94]

Though it may seem that others are choosing our habitation, it is our sovereign Lord who actually makes these choices, leading us from one place to another. He will turn each dreary dwelling place into a house of grace in which we can shed the light of God's lovingkindness on other travelers. And He will be our companion and friend until our traveling days are over and we reach our heart's true Home.

God of the coming years, through paths
unknown we follow *Thee.*

FROM THE GROUND UP

We descend by self-exaltation and ascend by humility.

—ST. BENEDICT

I read the other day of Charles Simeon, the nineteenth-century English preacher and leader of the evangelical revival in the Church of England. As an elderly man he was noted for his gentle, humble ways, but in his early years Simeon was proud and self-assertive.

One day he was visiting a friend, Henry Venn, who was pastor in the village of Yelling some miles away from Simeon's church in Cambridge. When he left to go home, Venn's daughters complained to their father about his manner.

Venn took the girls to the backyard and said, "Pick me one of those peaches." It was early summer, and the peaches were very green. The girls asked why he wanted the green, unripe fruit. Venn replied, "Well, my dears, it is green now, and we must wait; but a lit-

87

tle more sun, and a few more showers, and the peach will be ripe and sweet. So it is with Mr. Simeon."

Simeon, in due time, came to recognize his own arrogance. The warmth of God's love and the showers of opposition, misunderstanding, misrepresentation, disappointment, and frustration that fell upon him became the means by which he grew downward in humility and upward in adoration.

Thus the God of all grace works in the lives of His children, humbling the proud and exalting the humble, to make us ripe and sweet.

We imagine that spiritual growth is upward, when in fact the path to usefulness and maturity is a downward spiral through difficulty, contradiction, injustice, and humiliation. There is no other way. We must be brought low, rendered powerless, stripped of pretense and defensiveness. We must be left empty, insignificant, useless, feeling like dirt.

"Dirt" is exactly the right word, for fruitfulness grows from the ground up.[95] As Jesus said, "Unless a kernel of wheat falls to the ground and dies, it remains only a single seed. But if it dies, it produces many seeds."[96]

God brings us to ground, and aging is one of His means. Past sin, frailty, discomfort, physical decline, and thoughts of impending death all bring us down.

We must believe, then, that God is humbling us, that He is humbling us for a reason, and that He gives great grace to the humble.

The LORD sends poverty and wealth;
    he humbles and he exalts.
He raises the poor from the dust
    and lifts the needy from the ash heap;
he seats them with princes
    and has them inherit a throne of honor.[97]

Our part, in the midst of all that is happening to us, is to see God's grace in our frustrations and accept them as His loving hand upon us without growing weary or running away. We must take courage, and wait for the Lord to make us "ripe and sweet."

One of my favorite lines in all of C. S. Lewis's writings is found in his Narnia tale *The Horse and His Boy*. The great warhorse Bree, the "Horse" in the title, had humiliated himself by running away from battle. Now he thought he could never again show his face in Narnia and was stricken with terrible remorse over his cowardice.

"I've lost everything" he cried.

"My good Horse," said the Hermit of the Southern March, "you've lost nothing but your self-conceit. No, no, cousin. Don't put back your ears and shake your mane at me. If you are really so humbled as you sounded a minute ago, you must learn to listen to sense. You're not quite the great Horse you had come to think, from living among poor dumb horses. Of course you were braver and cleverer than them. You could hardly help being that. It doesn't follow that you'll be anyone very special in Narnia. But as long as you know you're nobody very special, you'll be a very decent sort of Horse, on the whole, and taking one thing with another."

THE HAND ON THE HELVE

And behind the working is a mind controlling,
And a force directing, and a guiding hand.
—ANNIE JOHNSON FLINT

A friend of mine tells me that he may have prostate cancer, but must wait for several months for a final diagnosis. "The Sword of Damocles is hanging over my head," he says.

Damocles, according to classical mythology, was a courtier who served King Dionysius, a fourth-century tyrannical ruler of the Greek colony of Syracuse. King Dionysius enjoyed all the blessings of power and wealth and seemed to be living the perfect life. Damocles would often compliment the king on his wealth and power. One day when he did this, the king asked if he would like to try living his life for a day. Damocles eagerly agreed and enjoyed himself immensely until he noticed a sharp sword suspended above his head by a single hair. This, Dionysius explained, was what life as a ruler was really like.[98]

"The Sword of Damocles," then, is an allusion to this tale and has become a symbol for any perilous situation in which tragedy is imminent and foreboding. My friend's comment, thus, takes on vivid meaning: He lives each day with the knowledge that his fate is hanging by the slenderest of threads.

As I thought about what my friend had told me, I suddenly saw *the hand* on the helve of the sword. The fate of my friend is not based on slender chance, miscalculation, or accident, but on the wisdom and goodness of the loving Father who holds the "sword," whatever it may be. My friend is in the strong hands of one who loves Him and cares for Him as no other can.

The Heidelberg Catechism asks: "What dost thou mean by the providence of God?" And answers: "The almighty and everywhere present power of God; whereby, as it were by His hand, He upholds and governs heaven, earth, and all creatures; so that herbs and grass, rain and drought, fruitful and barren years, meat and drink, health and sickness, riches and poverty, yea, and all things come, not by chance, but by His fatherly hand."

You and I may face terrifying circumstances in this life over which we have no control: rain or drought, fruitful or barren years, health or sickness, riches or poverty, life or death. These circumstances, when they come to us, may seem capricious and mere chance, but they are not. "The force that holds them, retards them, stops and starts and guides them, is our Father's hand."[99]

David knew this. "But you, O God, do see trouble and grief; you consider it to *take it in hand*. The victim commits himself to you."[100]

WHAT I MAKE OF IT

"Why, yes, Cephalus," said I, "and I enjoy talking with the very aged. For to my thinking we have to learn of them as it were from wayfarers who have preceded us on a road on which we too, it may be, must some time fare—what it is like—is it rough and hard-going or easy and pleasant to travel. And so now I would fain learn of you what you think of this thing, now that your time has come to it, the thing that the poets call 'the threshold of old age.' Is it a hard part of life to bear, or what report have you to make of it?"

—SOCRATES IN PLATO'S *THE REPUBLIC*

Socrates asks his friend Cephalus, a very old man, "Is [aging] a hard part of life to bear, or what report have you to make of it?"

Cephalus answers that he often gathers with older men whose complaints fill the air. They miss the pleasures of youth and regret them as if they had been robbed of great things. He, however, feels no regret and can't identify with their complaints, for he's enjoying old age.

"There is only one reason for what happens [to us as we age]," he explains. "[It is] not old age, but a man's character.[101] For if they [the aging] are decent, even-tempered people, old age is only moderately troublesome; if not then youth is no less difficult than age is for some people."[102]

In other words, it's not aging that makes life hard to bear, but unrighteousness, an idea Solomon underscores in his couplet: "The silver-haired head is a crown of glory, *if* it is found in the way of righteousness."[103]

It seems, then, old age can be "good old age," or it can be very bad. It all depends on the direction of one's life. The important thing is not to live long, but to live well. "Of what use is a long life if we amend so little?" wrote Thomas à Kempis. "Alas, a long life often adds to our sins rather than to our virtue."[104]

In my opinion, the first half of life is a piece of cake. The hard part comes later as our strength begins to decline. It's then that the stuff of which we're made begins to show. Folks can mask their bad behavior better when they're younger; they have the energy to do so. But when old age sets in, the restraints come off and they may become irascible, irritable, testy, and short-tempered (think *Grumpy Old Men*).

Those traits don't develop simply because people get older. Oh, there are conditions that cause confusion and anxiety as we age, but nothing in aging *necessarily* impairs us morally. No, I think as we grow older we finally become what we've been becoming all along.

Paul had a good word on the subject: "The one who sows to please his sinful nature [to please himself] . . . will reap destruction; the one who sows to please the Spirit . . . will reap eternal life."[105]

Those who pander to self-interest are sowing seeds that will inevitably produce a harvest of misery in themselves and in others. On the other hand, those who love God and others are sowing seeds that yield a harvest of life. Every day they're becoming more alive than ever before.

Old dogs *can* learn new tricks. There is a very real sense in which we can begin again. We can ask God to fill us again with *His* goodness. Every day can be a new beginning. We can mature, grow, and become sweeter as the days go by.

Listen:

> Lord, at Thy feet my prostrate heart is lying,
>> Worn with the burden, weary of the way;
> The world's proud sunshine on the hills is dying,
>> And morning's promise fades with parting day.
> Yet, in Thy light another morn is breaking,
>> Of fairer promise and with pledge more true;

And in Thy life a dawn of youth is waking,
   Whose bounding pulses shall this heart
   renew.

Oh, to go back across the years long vanished,
   To have the words unsaid, the deeds undone,
The errors cancelled, the deep shadows
   banished,
   In the glad sense of a new life begun.
To be a little child, whose page of story
   Is yet undimmed, unblotted by a stain,
And in the sunrise of primeval glory
   To know that life has had its start again.

I may go back across the years long vanished,
   I may resume my childhood, Lord, in Thee,
When in the shadow of Thy cross are banished
   All other shadows that encompass me:
And o'er the road that now is rough and dreary,
   This soul, made buoyant by a strength
   divine,
Shall walk untired, shall run and not be weary,
   To bear the blessings that have made Thee
   mine.[106]

I read the other day that Abraham was circum-
cised—the visible, outward sign of his covenant
love for God—when he was ninety-five years of age.
"Better late than never!" I say.

HANDICAPPED

> *God sometimes makes choice of those as his mes-*
> *sengers, who have the least of the advantages of*
> *art or nature, that his grace in them may appear*
> *the more glorious.*
>
> —MATTHEW HENRY
> COMMENTARY ON EXODUS 4:10–17

Years ago, in my student days (shortly after the earth's crust began to cool), I took a course in Ugaritic, the language of the ancient Canaanites. One day we were presented with a small tablet from a Canaanite temple. On it was a prayer, left at the feet of a musty old idol. It read, "O El, cut through the root of my stammering; remove the impediment." These were the words of an unfortunate Canaanite, humiliated by his affliction, imploring his god to remove his handicap.

Contrast the Canaanite El with our God—the Living God. While He may heal our handicaps, more often than not He takes them as they are and puts them to glorious use. Consider God's servant, Moses.

A Jewish legend says that Moses had a speech impediment. Recent studies suggest that the legend is accurate in that Moses' description of himself as "slow of speech and tongue"[107] is squarely in the realm of ancient medical terminology describing a speech defect. We have no way of knowing what Moses' defect was, but it must have been severe. Perhaps, like the frustrated Canaanite, he stuttered. Imagine Moses standing before the most powerful ruler in the ancient world and stammering his demand, "L-l-l-let my p-p-p-people g-g-go!"

God's answer to Moses' disclaimer is astonishing. "And who do you think made the human mouth? And who makes some mute, some deaf, some sighted, some blind? Isn't it I, God?" the Lord asks, thus explaining that impairments, disabilities, and handicaps are not accidents, but byproducts of God's infinite wisdom.[108] He creates every one of us *as we are*, and *uses* us *as we are*. His way of dealing with our handicaps is not necessarily to remove them, but to endow them with strength.

Here is one of the ironies of faith: God chooses those we least expect to do His holy work. It is the handicapped, the seemingly limited people, that astound the world.

Paul said of his handicap: "Three times I pleaded with the Lord to take it away from me. But he said to me, 'My grace is sufficient for you, for my power is made perfect in weakness.' Therefore," Paul concluded, "I will boast all the more gladly about my weaknesses, so that Christ's power may rest on me. That is why, for Christ's sake, I delight in weaknesses . . . For when I am weak, then I am strong."[109]

I have a friend who is dying of Parkinson's disease, who each month can do less than the month before. He was a tough and hardy soul who, in his former days, roamed the forests of Suriname and Brazil, often out of touch with the outside world for months at a time, looking for unreached people. Today he can do little more than smile.

But what a smile! His face is luminous with the love of Christ, and reveals a compassionate affection that warms the hearts of all who visit him. To be with him for a moment or two makes my day.

Is my friend handicapped? Oh no! God's strength is made perfect in his weakness.

PAYING ATTENTION

Hark! Hark! The dogs do bark,
The beggars are coming to town.
Some in rags and some in tags,
And one in a velvet gown.
— NURSERY RHYME

David wrote: "How blessed is he who *considers* the helpless [the poor]." His beatitude set me to thinking.

The poor we'll always have with us, Jesus said. Some are poor in possessions and appearance; others are poor in faith, hope, and love. Even if I can't alleviate the poverty of those I meet along the way, I can "consider" them—a verb that means "to pay attention."[110]

G. K. Chesterton defines a saint as one who exaggerates what the world neglects, and what is neglected today is the art of paying attention. Few seem to be aware of the pain around them; they go their way inattentive and unmoved.

In such a world it's not difficult to find some want to supply, some misery to alleviate. A divorcée or widow, grief-stricken in her loneliness. A weary parent kept awake at night by the struggles of a hurting child. A frightened man awaiting cancer surgery in the morning. A care-worn checker in a grocery store working a second or third job to make ends meet. A young boy who has never had enough father. A single mother whose flood of worries has washed her hope away. A lonely old man who has outlived his usefulness, or so he believes. A hurting heart behind your own front door. Perhaps we don't have much to give, but we can pay attention. We can see beyond what others see to the possibilities of mercy, compassion, and understanding.[111]

This past summer I came across a book entitled *The Singing Creek Where the Willows Grow* which contains the diary of a semi-literate twelve-year-old child who lived at the turn of the century in lumber camps in western Oregon. As I read Opal's diary I was awed by her simple compassion and sensitivity. Though often abused, she was not swallowed up in self-pity, but hid herself in God (as her poems indicate) and freely gave herself away. She was a happy child who teaches us what it means to "pay attention."

Here's a brief excerpt from her diary. I've included it as it is, though her vernacular may sound strange to our ears.

The mama did send me in a hurry to the wood-shed. It was for two loads of wood she wanted. I did bring in the first load in a hurry. The second load I brought not so. I did pick up all the sticks my arms could hold. While I was picking them up, I looked long looks at them. I went not to the kitchen with them in a quick way. I was meditating. I did have thinks about the tree they all were before they got chopped up. I did wonder how I would feel if I was a very little piece of wood that got chopped out of a big tree. I did think that it would have hurt my feelings. I felt the feelings of the wood. They did have a very sad feel.

Just when I was getting that topmost stick a bit wet with sympathy tears—then the mama did come up behind me with a switch. She said while she did switch, "Stop your meditations," and while she did switch, I did drop the wood. I felt the feels the sticks of wood felt when they hit the floor. Then I did pick them up with care and I put them all in the wood-box back of the cook stove. . . But all the time I was churning (the butter) I did hum a little song. It was a good-bye song to the sticks in the wood-box back of the kitchen stove.

When the churning was done and the butter was come, the mama did lift all the little lumps of butter out of the churn. Then she did pat them together in a big lump, and this she put away in the butterbox in the wood-shed. When she went to lay herself down to rest on the bed, she did call me to rub her head. I like to rub the mama's head, for it does help the worry lines to go away. Often I rub her head, for it is often she does have longings to have it so. And I do think it is very nice to help people have what they do have longings for.

So I, too, should be willing to bear the pain that brings me to Jesus who feels our feelings and rubs our worry lines away. So I, too, should take long looks at others.

I can let people know that I care. I can ask them to tell their stories and listen patiently while they do. I can treat them with courtesy and respect, though they may be testy or tiresome. I can encourage those with aching hearts with a word of God's mercy and love. I can follow up with an e-mail, a card, or a call. And I can pray with them, the most helpful and healing act of all, for in prayer I bring others to the throne of mercy where they may find grace to help in their time of need.[112] Even when I cannot help them, I can bring them to the One who can. And here's where David's beatitude comes into play, for in the oldest and oddest paradox of all, paying attention pays off, for we're happiest when we give our lives away.[113]

And for those who think only of themselves? The life they save is the life they lose. In the end it's worth nothing to anyone including themselves—a featureless, lifeless parody of those who have lived and cared for others. "Only a life given away for love's sake is worth living," says Fredrick Buechner.

> You will find as you look back upon your life that the moments that stand out, the moments when you have really lived, are the moments when you have done things in a spirit of love. As memory scans the past, above and beyond all transitory pleasures of life, there leap forward those supreme hours when you have been enabled to do unnoticed kindnesses to those around you, things too trifling to speak about, but which you feel have entered into your eternal life. I have seen almost all the beautiful things that God has made; I have enjoyed almost every pleasure that [God] has planned for [people]; and yet as I look back I see standing out above all the life that has gone four or five short experiences when the love of God reflected itself in some poor imitation, some small act of love of mine, and these seem to be things which alone of all one's life abide. Everything else in all our lives is transitory. Every other good is visionary. But the acts of love which no [one] knows about, or can ever know about, they never fail.[114]

The greatest thing in the world is love. It's our best gift to God and to others. Perhaps you and I can do nothing more than love *one* soul, but it is enough.

But what is left for the cold gray soul,
That moans like a wounded dove?
One wine is left in the broken bowl!—
'Tis—to love, and love, and love.

—George MacDonald, *Phantastes*

Habitual Tenderness

Gentleness may well be called the Christian spirit. It is the distinguishing disposition in the hearts of Christians to be identified as Christians. All who are truly godly have a gentle spirit in them.

—JONATHAN EDWARDS

One of the byproducts of aging can be an intolerance of others and an irritable, impatient spirit. We may become angry, bitter curmudgeons if we're not watchful. And when that happens . . .

All usefulness and all comfort may be prevented by an unkind, a sour, crabbed temper of mind—a mind that can bear with no difference of opinion or temperament. A spirit of fault-finding; an unsatisfied temper; a constant irritability; little inequalities in the look, the temper, or the manner; a brow cloudy and dissatisfied—your husband or your wife cannot tell why—will more than neutralize all the good you can do, and render life anything but a blessing.[115]

We must never excuse our bouts of bad temper, for intolerance spreads misery all around us and withers the souls of those we love. We have not fulfilled our duty toward others until we have learned to be pleasant.

Poet Hannah More portrays it this way:

Since trifles make the sum of human things,
And half our misery from our foibles springs;
Since life's best joys consist in peace and ease,
And though but few can serve, yet all can please;
Oh, let the ungentle spirit learn from hence,
A small unkindness is a great offence.

Ancient Greek philosophers had a word for the virtue that corrects our irritation—*praus*, a term that means gentleness and suggests a tender, kind spirit. It was considered the "queen of the virtues," for it governs and blesses all the others. It softens the sterner virtues and makes them more tender and gentle. Like sugar dropped into a cup of tea, it permeates our actions and sweetens all that we do. The author of the book of James, who understood the classical use of the word, describes the consummate good life as deeds done "in the meekness [gentleness, *prautes*] of wisdom."[116]

Gentleness is not weakness or mildness. Jesus was meek but not mild, despite Wesley's Christmas carol. Gentleness is strength under control. It is the power to be kind and considerate in the face of pain or disruption. It is a willingness to accept our limitations and ailments without taking out our frustrations on others. It is showing gratitude for the smallest service rendered to us and extending patience to those that do not serve us well. It is bearing with bothersome people (even noisy, boisterous little children, for kindness to little people is a crowning mark of a good and gentle soul).[117] It is speaking softly in the face of provocation.[118] It is even being silent, for calm, unruffled silence is often the most eloquent response to another's unkind words.

The root of a gentle spirit is humility. We must focus on our own weaknesses rather than the weakness and failures of others and their frustrating inability to wholly meet our needs. It is said that Israel's high priests were "able to deal gently with those who [were] ignorant and [were] going astray" because they themselves were "subject to weakness."[119] If I would be gentle and meek with those who disappoint me, I must know that I am as flawed and weak as they.

Since Jesus comes to me "gentle and riding on a donkey,"[120] I must get off my high horse and learn from Him, for He is "gentle [*praus*] and humble in heart,"[121] and He must create His likeness in me. Then who knows what will happen? Perhaps nothing will change but my own heart, and I will become a more gracious, gentle man. Or it may be that my gentle manner will open the eyes of someone else's heart, someone who has no gentle Jesus to see.

"Tones that jar the heart of another, words that make it ache . . . from such, as from all other sins, Jesus was born to deliver us," George MacDonald prayed. May we put ourselves into His hands for His healing.

WEARINESS

More life I need ere I myself can be.
Sometimes, when the eternal tide ebbs low,
A moment weary of my life I grow.
—GEORGE MACDONALD, *DIARY OF AN OLD SOUL*

What is this weariness that settles upon us as we age? Does it come from something that needs to be set right?

Not necessarily. Sin does wear us out. The burden of guilt and shame is a heavy load to bear. But it may not be evil-doing that weighs us down. We may be "weary in well-doing," as Paul would say, for love can be hard work that wears out both body and soul. Or, our weariness may be the sin of another and our inability to give help as we would like to do. Or it may come simply from prolonged illness or pain.

I delight in George MacDonald's *Diary of an Old Soul,* for my old soul resonates so readily with his. There he writes:

Shall fruit be blamed if it hang wearily
A day before it perfected drop plumb
To the sad earth from off its nursing tree?
Ripeness must always come with loss of might.
The weary evening fall before the resting night.[122]

Weariness and "loss of might" bring ripeness, for they remind us that we're passing away so that a better thing may come. The weary evening leads to the resting night. This is what we Christians call "hope," and in this hope we renew our souls, as the prophet Isaiah declares.

[Our] Lord is the everlasting God,
      the Creator of the ends of the earth.
He will not grow tired or weary,
      and his understanding no one can fathom.
He gives strength to the weary
      and increases the power of the weak.
Even youths grow tired and weary,
      and young men stumble and fall;
but those who hope in the Lord
      will renew their strength.
They will soar on wings like eagles;
      they will run and not grow weary,
      they will walk and not be faint.[123]

Hope, Isaiah's strong word, looks to the future. It is waiting in confidence for a salvation that is certain to come—kept in heaven for those who are themselves kept for the day of salvation.

This is the perspective that overwhelms my weariness; not accidentally, but essentially, for if I know that my ultimate destiny is glorious, it picks up my pace here and now. I can stretch the wings of my heart and fly! I can run in the path of obedience and not get tired. I can walk through routine, pedestrian days and not grow weary.

The spirit is willing, but the flesh is weak, I say; but a better world is coming in which my spirit will call me to action and my body will run and leap and fly! This is my assurance, for hope, in biblical terms, does not imply contingency but certainty. As a back-country friend of mine once put it, "My salvation is for certain sure!"

In the meantime, what someday will be true can begin to be true even now. I can be steadfast, patient, and joyful in spite of my deep weariness; kind and calm, less focused on my own frailty and fatigue; more concerned about others than I am about my-self—and thus able "to speak a word in season to him that is weary."[124]

So MacDonald prays,

I am a little weary of my life—
Not thy life, blessed Father! Or the blood
Too slowly laves the coral shores of thought,
Or I am weary of weariness and strife.[125]

Open my soul-gates to thy living flood;
I ask not larger heart-throbs, vigor–fraught,
I pray thy presence, with strong patience rife.

STUFF

Happiness is neither outside nor inside us; it is in
God, both outside and inside us.
—BLAISE PASCAL, PENSÉES

I was rummaging around in my son's garage some
months ago and came across a box containing the
trophies he'd won during his years of athletic compe-
tition. There they were, abandoned and laden with
dust, about to be carted away. I thought of the discipline and effort that had gone into gaining those
treasures, and how much my son had once valued
them. But now they meant nothing to him. They were
trash.

Then I thought of all the stuff I've accumulated
through the years—things in closets, boxes, and
storage bins. "Things upon the mantle, things on every shelf, things that others gave me, things I gave
myself."[126]

Every year my possessions accumulate and clut-
ter my existence more and more. The thought of mov-

ing it all or discarding it fills me with dread. It's just "stuff." I wish I'd never collected it.

Shel Silverstein, a writer of children's verses, makes a similar point in a whimsical poem he entitles "Hector the Collector." In it he describes the objects Hector accumulated over the years and how he "Loved these things with all his soul, / Loved them more than shining diamonds, / Loved them more than glistenin' gold." Then Hector called to all the people, "'Come and share my treasure trunk!'" They "came and looked . . . and called it junk."[127]

So it will be in the end. All the things that you and I have accumulated will be rubbish.

Still we continually seek more "stuff," for we've been deceived into believing that acquisition and accumulation lead to happiness. All day long voices urge us to buy this, spend for that, borrow against tomorrow so we can have what we want today. Generous incentives, rebates, sales packages, low or no interest rates, and other "good deals" lure us on, creating wants in us that we never imagined. The belief that "just one more thing" will make us happy lingers in our minds.

We gather, harbor, and store things until we have no places to put them. Yet we must always have more, what a friend of mine calls, The Barbie Doll Law: Accessories once considered optional become mandatory, creating needs and wants never had before. Things that used to be add-ons become must-haves— a limitless multiplication of unnecessary necessities.

In our quest for all our doodads, gimcracks, and gewgaws, we buy well beyond our ability to pay. The only limiting factor is our imagination and credit card limit, which can always be extended.

Yet though we buy (and buy, and buy) enough is never enough. We must have one more gadget, or its upgrade, a compulsion that has no cure on earth.

But there is healing from above. The happiness we are seeking in all our "getting" is truly found only in loving and being loved by God. "Blessed are those you choose and bring near . . . We are filled with the good things of your house. . ."[128] In His love we find full satisfaction.

Indeed, all our wanting and getting is nothing more than a symptom of the heart's deepest desire— the desire for God himself. We were made to be filled and flooded with God *alone*; there is thus an infinite space within us that no number of toys or other joys can fill. Only infinite Love will do.

God is not just one more good thing among others. He is the cause of all good, the "giver of every good and perfect gift"—the source of "the good life" and the happiness we seek.

"One who has God has everything," Augustine wrote. "And one who has everything except God has nothing. And one who has God plus everything has no more than one who has God alone."

Another of Israel's poets put the same idea this way: "Earth has nothing I desire besides you . . . God

is the strength of my heart and my portion forever
. . . it is good to be near God."[129]

The greatest thing in the world is to know that
God loves us. He is our Father and we are His beloved. The second greatest thing is *to know that we
need nothing more.* Then, and only then, can we say,
"I shall not want."[130]

A River Runs through Us

I read in an Old fashioned Book
That People "thirst no more"—
—EMILY DICKINSON

I love to stroll alongside Idaho's brooks and streams that run like veins of silver through this beautiful land. But in all my days—and I've been around awhile—I've never seen a river like the one Ezekiel saw.[131]

The prophet, in a vision, was touring the temple in Jerusalem, accompanied by an angelic companion, when he came upon a rivulet flowing from under the threshold of the temple—just a trickle. Ezekiel traced the tiny stream to its source and discovered a spring bubbling up from the ground from under the brazen altar, the place of sacrifice.

Ezekiel's companion then led him outside the walls of the city and downstream to the place where the river flowed off the flanks of Mount Zion toward the east. The angel had a measuring stick in his hand, and as he walked he measured off the distance.

Ezekiel and his friend walked a little less than a quarter of a mile, and the angel led Ezekiel into the water. It was ankle-deep.

The angel then paced off the same distance and led Ezekiel into the water. It was knee-deep.

He measured off the distance again and led Ezekiel into the river. The water was up to his waist.

The angel measured off the distance and led Ezekiel into the river again. The water was over his head, a river "deep enough to swim in—a river that no-one could cross."

Then Ezekiel saw the region to which the river flowed: a dead sea that was made alive! Great schools of fish were swimming in its waters; fishermen were crowding its banks; trees were growing in profusion along its shores—"because the water from the sanctuary flows to them."

First a sanctuary, then an altar, and then a stream trickling out from under the altar that gets wider and deeper as it flows—an inexhaustible, copious supply that takes away bitterness and makes the land sweet and fruitful. All because a river flows through it.

There are no rivers on earth like Ezekiel's stream—no streams that begin as a trickle and get wider and deeper without tributaries or underground springs. We ask ourselves, as Ezekiel's companion asked, "Do you *see* this?"

If we take the trouble to trace the little stream

to its source, we find an altar, a place of sacrifice on which the Lamb of God was slain. Underneath the altar there is a spring that bubbles up from the ground, a hidden source, a fountain of life.

Jesus said, "If anyone is thirsty, let him come to me and drink. Whoever believes in me, as the Scripture has said, streams of living water will flow from within him."[132] He alone is the living water for which we thirst, a fountain in the heart that becomes a river that flows deep and wide, a river that rises and floods, that empties into *our* dead seas, that dispels our dearth, filling our days with singing and laughter. "Where the river flows there is life!"

Are you weary in your love? Do you need new tenderness, compassion, and concern for those around you? Stoop down and drink from the hidden springs of God's love. Deepen your union with Him by prayer and devotion. He will be a spring of living water, of enduring, self-effacing love, rising up in you.

Are there demands on your time and energy that drain you until you have nothing left to give? Keep opening your heart to God. Pray over His Word and meditate on it day and night. New thoughts will spring up, fruit for food and leaves for healing. All your *fresh* springs are in Him.[133]

Are you weary of the struggle in your spiritual life? Do you seek a quiet, more restful progress, or a refreshment for the wilderness and waste places of your life? This too comes from God, for the life we live is not ours, but His. He is in us, a never-ending source of righteousness, joy, and peace. "Where [God's] river flows there is life!" There is no other source.

In C. S. Lewis's *The Silver Chair*, Jill finds herself lost and very thirsty, and looking for a stream. She finds a brook, but she also finds the lion, Aslan, lying beside it. Aslan assures her she may come and drink.

> "May I—could I—would you mind going away while I [drink]" said Jill.
>
> The Lion answered this only by a look and a very low growl. And as Jill gazed at its motionless bulk, she realized that she might as well have asked the whole mountain to move aside for her convenience.
>
> The delicious rippling noise of the stream was driving her nearly frantic.
>
> "Will you promise not to—do anything to me, if I do come" said Jill.
>
> "I make no promise," said the Lion.
>
> Jill was so thirsty now that, without noticing it, she had come a step nearer.
>
> "*Do* you eat girls?" she said.
>
> "I have swallowed up girls and boys, women and men, kings and emperors, cities and realms," said the Lion. It didn't say this as if it were boasting, nor as if it were sorry, nor as if it were angry. It just said it.

"I daren't come and drink," said Jill.

"Then you will die of thirst," said the Lion.

"Oh, dear!" said Jill, coming another step nearer. "I suppose I must go and look for another stream then."

"There is no other stream," said the Lion.[134]

"Whoever is thirsty, let him come; and whoever wishes, let him take the free gift of the water of life."[135] There is no cost, for Love paid the price on Calvary. There is only one requirement: We must *thirst*. Everyone who thirsts,

> Come to the waters;
> And you who have no money,
> Come, buy and eat.
> Yes, come, buy wine and milk
> Without money and without price.

> Why do you spend money for what is not bread,
> And your wages for what does not satisfy?
> Listen carefully to Me, and eat what is good,
> And let your soul delight itself in abundance.[136]

THE SOUND OF SILENCE

Ultimate peace is silent through the density of life. [137]

—C. S. LEWIS

Silence, I've come to believe, is the answer to many of life's contradictions, so I'm learning to say less these days.

Silence was often our Lord's way. In the face of severe provocation He "remained silent and gave no answer."[138] Jesus could have answered His critics, but "like a sheep that is silent before its shearers, so He did not open His mouth."[139]

There is awesome power in silence, especially in those overwhelmingly bad situations in which we are subject to harsh words from those we love. There, however, silence is most difficult, for loved ones have the greatest power to wound us. Yet there silence is most essential, for we owe our own loved ones the greatest measure of forbearance.

Silence forestalls angry reactions and bitter words

that we may later regret and others may not forget. Silence gives us time to slow our thoughts and reorder them, perhaps to remind ourselves that the one who wounded us is weary, or worried, or otherwise out of sorts. Silence gives us time to forgive.

Silence is also a means by which we may help others see themselves. As their voices reverberate in the quietness we offer, they may hear their unkind words and regret them. When we step aside and wait in stillness, we give God an opportunity to work through us. When we take up our own cause, we may frustrate His ultimate intention to use us to bring spiritual healing and health to others.

Silence can be the gentle answer that turns away anger.[140] Defensive reactions make things worse: they stir up anger. Restraint and silence relieve tension and restore peace. As James assures us, "Peacemakers who sow in peace raise a harvest of righteousness."[141] Others begin to grow toward goodness through our example.

Finally, calm, unruffled silence is an eloquent and gracious reflection of God's unconditional love. Clement, a first-century Christian, wrote, "Let [those who belong to Christ] demonstrate by silence the gentleness of their tongue; [and thus] let them show His love."[142]

The Good, the Better, the Best

*Now let me tell you that the will of God is all that
is necessary, and what it does not give you is of
no use to you at all. My friends, you lack nothing.
You would be very ashamed if you knew what the
experiences you call setbacks, upheavals, point-
less disturbances, and tedious annoyances really
are. You would realize that your complaints about
them are nothing more nor less than blasphe-
mies—though that never occurs to you. Nothing
happens to you except by the will of God, and yet
[God's] beloved children curse it because they do
not know it for what it is.*

— JEAN-PIERRE DE CAUSSADE,
ABANDONMENT TO DIVINE PROVIDENCE

King David fled from Jerusalem, forced out by a
disloyal son.[143] Feigning allegiance to his father,
Absalom had gathered an army of supporters and
was marching against the city to seize control of the

throne. David withdrew to spare his people the horrors of a prolonged siege.

David's calamities accumulated as he retreated. He discovered that his trusted friend and wise counselor, Ahithophel, had betrayed him. He was forced to send his loyal friend, Hushai, back to Jerusalem because he was too old to endure the rigors of a forced march. He was told that Mephibosheth, to whom David had shown great kindness, was among the conspirators.

For the sake of his people, David sent Zadok, his beloved priest and loyal friend, back to Jerusalem with the ark of God. With the departure of the ark, David mused, "If I find favor in the LORD's eyes, he will bring me back and let me see it and his dwelling place again." But if not, "then I am ready; let him do to me whatever seems good to him."[144]

Perhaps, like David, you have lost control of your life. Your home, your finances, your freedom, your future now lie in hands other than your own. Someone—perhaps someone you loved and trusted—has taken control, *or so it seems.*

You need to remember that even if power has been wrested from your hands, there are other hands at work. Behind every human act lies the action of One whose will is indomitable and whose power is supreme. He gives and takes what He will, when He wills it. He is the High King of heaven! No one can act without His permission; no one can frustrate His control.

"What do you understand by the providence of God?" the Heidelberg Catechism asks, then answers: "God's providence is the almighty and ever-present power, whereby, as with His own hand, He still upholds heaven and earth and all creatures, and so governs them that leaf and blade, rain and drought, fruitful and barren years, food and drink, health and sickness, riches and poverty, indeed all things come not by chance but by His fatherly hand."[145]

It is not human caprice that has overturned your plans, but God's sovereign will, for nothing and no one can frustrate His loving intention toward you and His resolve to bring eternal gain out of displacement and the loss of earthly possessions.

Tertullian, a third-century Christian, wrote, "[Do not regret] a thing which has been taken away, and taken away by the Lord God, without whose will neither does a leaf glide down from a tree, nor a sparrow of one farthing's worth fall to the earth."[146]

God's ways are too deep, too lofty, too wise for us to understand, but we can know that His will is "good, pleasing, and perfect."[147] Perfect, because His plan is greater than mere preservation of our goods. It is to make us good children—gracious in loss and upheaval, confident in our heavenly Father's prudence and care, peaceful in the certainty of His love.

But this goodness grows from acceptance, because we cannot know that God's will is good and perfect, and we will not find it pleasing, until we have offered up our privileges, possessions, our circumstances—indeed *ourselves*—to God.[148] We must dare to look up to Him and say, "I accept this circumstance and all I have lost as you have planned it. I refuse nothing that seems good to you."

Thus we echo David's words: "I am ready; let [God] do to me whatever seems good to him," and put ourselves in His fatherly hands.

> To have, each day, the thing I wish,
> Lord, that seems best to me;
> But not to have the thing I wish,
> Lord, that seems best to Thee.
> Most truly, then, Thy will is done,
> When mine, O Lord, is crossed;
> It is good to see my plans o'erthrown,
> My ways in Thine all lost.

—Horatio Bonar

Fresh Starts

Time was, I shrank from what was right,
From fear of what was wrong;
I would not brave the sacred fight,
Because the foe was strong.

But now I cast that finer sense
And sorer shame aside;
Such dread of sin was indolence,
Such aim at heaven was pride.
—JOHN HENRY NEWMAN

I read Stephan Donaldson's *Lord Foul's Bane* last summer, the first volume of *The Chronicles of Thomas Covenant the Unbeliever,* in which Donaldson tells the story of Thomas Covenant, a young novelist who is inexplicably stricken with leprosy. Although his leprosy is eventually arrested, he's taught that his only hope of survival lies in scrupulous visual self-examination.

Covenant is devastated when his wife abandons and divorces him to protect their son from exposure.

Furthermore, people around him cast him in the traditional role of a leper: unclean, outcast, unwanted. Unable to write, he struggles to go on living; and as the pressure of his loneliness mounts, he begins to experience episodes of unconsciousness during which he enters an alternative world known as "the Land."

In the Land, Covenant is fully healed and is greeted as the reincarnation of an ancient hero known as Berek Halfhand. But because he refuses to believe that he has been cured and believes himself tainted and destroyed, Covenant can do nothing for the Land and its people.

The Land has an ancient enemy, Lord Foul the Despiser. Against him stands the Council of Lords, who have dedicated their lives to acquiring the wisdom by which they may stave off his attacks. Yet Thomas is unable to take up his call to face Lord Foul the Despiser and can only give half-hearted support to the council as he bargains his way out of involvement. He is paralyzed by his inability to accept the fact that he has been made thoroughly clean. He is controlled by his unbelief.

I know folks like Thomas—downcast in their sins, struggling in the discouragement and lethargy that grows from over-scrupulous self-examination and morbid fixation with their own sin and guilt.[149] Some have given up on themselves and have withdrawn into inertia and isolation. They do little more than watch television, sleep, and eat three meals a day.

I like to remind these dear folks of Peter's three-fold denial and subsequent encounter with Jesus on that beach by the Sea of Galilee. Think of Jesus' cordial greeting to Peter, the warmth of the fire, the hearty meal—*and no mention of Peter's failure.*[150]

"Do you love me, Peter?" Jesus asked.

Peter, humbled by denial and defeat, could only murmur, "You know that I love you, Lord."

Jesus answered, "Go feed my sheep."

It may be that some of us, humiliated by sin and failure, like Peter, question our credibility as Christians. We minutely scrutinize our souls and find ungodliness, and wonder if our struggle with sin has disqualified us and rendered us useless.

The answer is that sin itself does not disqualify us. Forgiveness and renewal are always at hand if we are truly repentant. George MacDonald said that the man or woman "Who, after failure, or a poor success, / Rises up, stronger effort yet renewing—He finds thee, Lord, at length, in his own common room."[151] When we turn from our sin and ask for His help, our Lord is there to welcome us and lift us up.

Repentance, of course, is the essential element. We must be "converted," to use Jesus' word: We must hate our sin, turn from it, and ask for our Lord's forgiveness.[152] We must rise from our fall and begin again. Then, like Peter, full of our Savior's affirmation, we can strengthen our brothers.

It comes to me that what God is after is not perfection (that awaits heaven), but the humility that comes from self-awareness. Failure cures us of our illusion of near-perfection—"aiming at heaven," John Henry Newman would say. "We learn, on the one hand, that we cannot trust ourselves even in our best moments, and, on the other, that we need not despair even in our worst, for our failures are forgiven."[153]

We should, of course, strive for "moral excellence," the standard of goodness in the ancient world and Peter's first-rate word,[154] but we must be content with occasional failure. And we must be patient while God himself chooses and works at those aspects of our character that give *Him* the greatest pleasure.[155] In time He will deal with all that shames us.

> If someone falls into some error, he does not fret over it, but rising up with a humble spirit, he goes on his way anew rejoicing. Were he to fall a hundred times in the day, he would not despair—he would rather cry out lovingly to God, appealing to His tender pity. The really devout man has a horror of evil, but he has a still greater love of that which is good; he is more set on doing what is right than avoiding what is wrong. Generous, large-hearted, he is not afraid of danger in serving God, and would rather run the risk of doing His will imperfectly than not strive to serve Him lest he fail in the attempt.[156]

Jesus, as always, has the last word: "I've prayed for you in particular that you not give in or give out. When you have come through the time of testing, turn to your companions and give *them* a fresh start."[157]

RATS!

May I, composed like them
Of Eros and of dust,
Beleaguered by the same
Negation and despair,
Show an affirming flame.
    —W. H. AUDEN, "SEPTEMBER 1, 1939"

I have a friend who has a barn on her farm in which she stores a large quantity of grain. The barn is a handsome structure, well-built, immaculately maintained—and infested with rats! You don't see the beasts in the daylight because they hide, but in the dark they come out to feed and spoil the grain. Turn on the lights suddenly and step into the room and you see them clearly—just before they scamper away to their holes.

C. S. Lewis takes a lesson from the same observation: "If there are rats in a cellar you are most likely to see them if you go in very suddenly. But the suddenness does not create the rats: it only prevents them from hiding. In the same way the suddenness of the provocation does not make me an ill-tempered man; it only shows me what an ill-tempered man I am. The rats are always there in the cellar, but if you go in shouting and noisily they will have taken cover before you switch on the light."[158]

In other words, my behavior, when caught off guard, is the best evidence of the sort of person I am. That being the case, I should never excuse my bad behavior simply because I'm suddenly prodded or provoked. What I am under unexpected pressure is what I am. There's no way around it.

It occurs to me that I would be a much better person—or at least would appear to be better— if I could control all my circumstances, or if my circumstances always favored me. But I live in a world that cannot be ruled or controlled, and surprise is the name of the game. Someone or something always jars me unexpectedly and I find myself to be a curmudgeon.

Of all my sins—and they are legion—it's these autonomic sins that bother me most. Just when I think I'm making progress, some embarrassing display makes me believe I've made little or no progress at all. "It's enough to get a body down," as my mother used to say.

What I need to remember is that my sins, even those over which I seem to have no control, no matter how "Augean," are abundantly forgiven, washed away by the blood of the Lamb. They'll never be held against me.

Some years ago I read the myth of Augeas and discovered the derivation of that word "Augean." I knew it meant disgustingly filthy and difficult to cleanse, but I never knew its origin.

Augeas, according to the myth, was the king of Elis, a city-state on the west coast of Peloponnesus, the peninsula forming the southern part of Greece. He owned a stable that contained 3,000 oxen whose stalls hadn't been cleaned for 30 years. Imagine the filth and the smell!

As the legend goes, Hercules, who had to atone for the murder of his wife and children, was forced to perform ten labors, one of which was to clean the Augean stables in a single day. "If you don't complete the task," he was warned, "you will live in the stables and clean them for the rest of your life." Since Hercules was immortal, he was looking at a long stretch of mucking out.

When Hercules saw the stables he was dismayed by the size, the filthiness and stench. But then he noticed that the stables were located between two large rivers. He put his great strength to work and diverted the courses of the rivers so that they flowed through the stables. Within moments they were swept clean.

The story is a myth, of course, but myths by their nature preserve the yearnings of the cultures that embrace and perpetuate them. And the Augean stables offer a reflection of our own longing for someone to wash from our lives the accumulated waste and filth of the years, the memory . . .

> Of all that we have done, and been; the shame
> Of motives late revealed, and the awareness
> Of things ill done and done to others' harm . . .[159]

"What can wash away my sin?" asks the hymn writer. "Nothing but the blood of Jesus." No defilement, however Augean, can withstand it. When sin is humbly confessed, our Savior is faithful and just to forgive our sins and cleanse us from *all* unrighteousness.

But, I ask myself, must I still be saddled with sinful outbursts to the end of my days? No, there will be change, though it will not come swiftly or easily.

For myself, I find the business of sanctification confusing and chaotic rather than a straight line of progress. "Sometimes I'm up; sometimes I'm down," I lament with the spiritual. You would think after almost seventy-five years of being Christian I'd finally get things right, but there are still "rats" that hide in the darkness of my unfinished soul. Yet it's at times of greatest failure that I find it most consoling to realize that change is certain—God has promised it—even though it will always be slow, and partial, and there will be times when I appear to be slipping back. This humbles me and keeps me utterly dependent and clinging to God—which, in the end, may be more important to God than earthly perfection.

Only one thing is necessary, and that's faith—the faith to believe that not even my worst behavior can sever me from God's tenacious love. For God is a master workman who never abandons His projects or leaves them unfinished.

Our work is to long for holiness and to pray for it. God's work is to perfect us at His own pace and in His own way. And He will not give up on any of us until His work is done.

> Almighty and most merciful Father, whose clemency I now presume to implore, after a long life of carelessness and wickedness, have mercy upon me. I have committed many trespasses; I have neglected many duties. I have done what Thou hast forbidden, and left undone what Thou hast commanded. Forgive, merciful Lord, my sins, negligences, and ignorances, and enable me, by the Holy Spirit, to amend my life according to thy Holy Word, for Jesus Christ's sake. Amen.
>
> —From Doctor Johnson's Prayers

Things I Do Not Know

Satan has the intention of detaining us with unnecessary things and thus keeping us from those
that are necessary. Once he has gained an opening
in you of a handbreadth, he will force in his whole
body together with sacks full of useless questions.
—MARTIN LUTHER, INSTRUCTION FROM THE
SAINTS TO THE CHURCH IN ERFURT (1522)

I was looking at some of the clever, wonderful, un-
used books on my library shelves the other day and
thinking back to a time when, as a much younger
man, I envisioned myself spending twenty years or
so of my life ramping up my theological knowledge,
and then another twenty getting that knowledge or-
ganized. The demonstrable, the provable, the defin-
able loomed large in my mind.

As I've gotten older, however, I've learned to be
more comfortable with what I don't know and will
never know until I get to heaven. Like Israel's poet,
I no longer "concern myself with . . . things too won-

derful for me.[160] I find myself more open to mystery and uncertainty these days; I'm able to embrace more ambiguity.[161] My questions are rarely true or false, but multiple choice. I believe more ardently now than ever before, but in fewer and fewer things.

There are things I believe with all my heart—the Apostles' Creed wraps up most of them—but other, more remote aspects of theology that once dominated my thoughts don't weigh on my mind any more. G. K. Chesterton said that angels fly because they take themselves lightly. I'm trying to learn how to fly.

The main thing for me now is not to know all the answers, but to know God, made real and personal in Jesus. I pray for David's spirit, his quiet soul.[162] I find that few things are necessary now, really "only one."[163]

A by-product of this shift is that I no longer have the urge to mold people to my theological presuppositions. I can be more tolerant of those that disagree with me; I can let them be.[164] I also find myself more open to Christians who are not *exactly* my kind. It's with "all the saints" that we know all the dimensions of God's love, Paul reminds us.[165] I can learn from all of them.

Something happened to me some years ago that reinforced my thinking along these lines. I was a student then at the Graduate Theological Union, a consortium of seminaries in Berkeley, California. One of the schools was a seminary in which Jesuit priests are prepared. Though not Roman Catholic, I took most of my classes there.

One winter I enrolled in a tutorial with Dr. John Huesman, a Jesuit priest and ranking Hebrew scholar. I expected to learn from Fr. Huesman, but I learned a good deal more than I expected.

One cold, windy afternoon we were sitting at the kitchen table in his tiny apartment reading Isaiah 53. As I began to read the text, I looked into the good doctor's eyes, saw them glisten and tears begin to flow. He was weeping, not over my translation (which doubtlessly grieved him), but over the text.

"David," I said to myself, "you've read these words many times, but not once have you wept over them. You have much to learn from this man."

Ralph Waldo Emerson said, "Every man I meet is in some way my superior; in that I can learn from him." This is especially true of those whom God calls His own. I can learn from them, even if they're not *exactly* my kind.

The Hill Difficulty

He who has compassion on them will guide them
and lead them beside springs of water.
—ISAIAH 49:10

There is a glacial lake that lies high in a fold of Jug Handle Peak in the mountains north of our home in Boise. It's a dot on the map, but a place of rare beauty and tranquility for me.

The route to the lake takes me up a steep, exposed ridge through boulders and scree. It's a strenuous ascent—hard on my old heart and legs. In the summer, the sun beats down mercilessly on my head, and there's no shade to be found anywhere. At the bottom of the climb, however, there's a brook—a spring that seeps out of soft, mossy earth and flows through a lush meadow crammed with flowers that bloom in wild profusion. It's a quiet place to hydrate myself and prepare for the hard climb that lies ahead.

This reminds me of the moment in *The Pilgrim's Progress* when Christian and his fellow-travelers

143

find themselves at the foot of another steep ascent, the Hill Difficulty, at the bottom of which there is a spring. "Christian now went to the spring and drank thereof to refresh himself, and then began to go up the hill."[166]

Perhaps you, too, stand at the foot of Hill Difficulty facing an impossibly high mountain to be climbed, a challenge that cannot be met through mere strength or wisdom. Perhaps your mountain is the care of an aging or disabled spouse, a difficult financial decision—one on which your earthly future depends—or a painful recovery from a surgical procedure. The demands seem insurmountable.

Before you do anything else, visit the spring that is God himself. Come to Him with all your weakness, weariness, helplessness, failure, doubt, and fear. Drink deeply of His power and wisdom; fill yourself full of His everlasting love. (Dehydration imperils the body *and* soul.) Ask for faith and hardy endurance to face and surmount the difficulty. (To ask is to receive.)

Whatever we have to do, God must perfect it. He knows all our circumstances and supplies us *ahead of time* with a store of comfort, of spiritual strengthening and consolation, that we may have ready at hand, that we can resort to and lay up in our heart as an antidote against despair.[167]

We drink from the spring from which our Lord himself drank when He stood at the foot of Hill

Calvary—"a brook beside the way."[168] Then, rested and refreshed, having set the Lord before us, we can rise and face the difficulty that looms ahead.

The mountain may remain, as demanding as ever. But forearmed with prevenient grace—God's goodness and mercy that precedes all human effort—we can ascend with steady faith, hope, and love.

A RUIN! A RUIN! A RUIN!

He took the silver and the gold,
To make me rich in grace;
He quenched earth's lights that I might see
The shining of his face.

—F. B. MEYER

I was hiking in the mountains south of our home in Boise several months ago and came across the ruins of the Golden Chariot Mine, one of the richest gold mines in the Owyhee Mountains of Idaho. I had read that it was the cause of a bitter war that raged underground for weeks—a bloody gun battle in which a number of men lost their lives. The gold still lies in a rich vein that runs under War Eagle Mountain, yet the mine, and all that men gave their lives for there, remains in ruins.

"A ruin! A ruin! I will make it a ruin," Ezekiel exclaims, using the strongest superlative in the Hebrew language. "It will not be restored until he comes to whom it rightfully belongs."[169]

This prophecy was directed against Zedekiah, the king of Judah, and was a prediction of the siege of Jerusalem and its destruction by Nebuchadnezzar and his army.

Jerusalem was impregnable, or so Zedekiah believed, his place of ultimate safety. Its walls would never fall. Yet, as the prophecy foretold, the city in which he placed his trust would be reduced to ruins and would not be fully restored, "until He comes to whom it rightfully belongs."

This reference goes back a thousand years or more to Jacob's ancient prophecy: "The scepter will not depart from Judah, nor the ruler's staff from between his feet, *until he comes to whom it belongs* and the obedience of the nations is his."[170] This is the promise of Israel's Messiah, the one to whom the kingdom rightfully belonged. It was this reminder and the destruction of the city of Jerusalem that awakened God's people once again to their need for His wise and righteous rule and His promise that He would restore the city's glory and beauty.

Ruin comes to all of us so that God may build a better thing. He shakes what can be shaken, so that what cannot be shaken may remain. This is the hidden meaning of the devastation that brings down the things we've given our lives to build up and to maintain.

When we fall into ruin, God has graciously provided a way to rebuild. We may live with the results of our sin, but sin repented of draws us back into God's great heart and enables Him to restore us. The grace of men is a sometime thing; the grace of God endures forever.

God's grace is determined by His interest in us. He uses everything for *our* greater good, even our ruin. This is what theologians call "the economy of salvation." God wastes nothing, not even our sin. "God knows how to draw glory even from our faults. Not to be downcast after committing a fault is one of the marks of true sanctity."[171]

We must not let our defeats defeat us, for our defilement and God's forgiving grace can become the means by which we are drawn into an intimacy with our Lord in greater measure than before. Our sin—repented of and put away—can result in greater results for the kingdom of God than anything we could have accomplished otherwise. Grace takes our most depraved and black-hearted sin and turns it into something beautiful for Him. That, and not our sin, is the final word.

God rids our hearts of past sorrow, even as His goodness and love treat our sins as if they had never happened. And then, as David assures us, "He leads us in paths of righteousness."

The retirement funds we've accumulated with so much care are lost that we may acquire better riches. The reputation we've established for integrity and restraint is shattered that we may despair of our own goodness and find our righteousness in Christ. The friendships we've cultivated lie in ruins that we may gain a truer Friend. The love of our life is taken away that a greater Love may possess us. And then there is aging, the thing that eventually ruins all of us. We are brought down, rendered useless, stripped of pretense and defenses so God can build from the ground up. As George MacDonald said, we learn "to live without earthly provision or precaution." God becomes our sole good, the only thing we desire.

In the end our ruination will have become the best thing that ever happened to us, for it will have turned us to the One to whom we rightfully belong— and in so doing we are restored.

> I am alone in the dark, and I am thinking
> what darkness would be mine if I could see
> the ruin I wrought in every place I wandered
> and if I could not be aware of One who follows
>   after me.
> Whom do I love, O God, when I love Thee?
> The great Undoer who has torn apart
> the walls I built against a human heart,
> the Mender who has sewn together the hedges
> through which I broke when I went seeking ill,
> the Love who follows and forgives me still.
> Fumbler and fool that I am, with things around
>   me
> and of fragile make like souls, how I am blessed

to hear behind me footsteps of a Savior!
I sing to the east, I sing to the lighted west:
God is my repairer of fences, turning my paths
    into rest.
—Jessica Powers, "Repairer of Fences" (Isaiah 58:12)

THE DISCIPLINE OF DISTRESS

If "the nightingale sings best with a thorn against
her breast," why not we?

—SUSAN GILBERT DICKINSON IN A LETTER

TO EMILY DICKINSON (1861)

Suffering is exact. We don't grieve in general or in the abstract, but in specific, concrete ways. Most of the consolation we receive, however, is loaded with generalizations and abstractions, as anyone who has ever received a sympathy card knows. "It's all for the best," our friends assure us. Or, "It will turn out for good."

Such comfort, however well-meant, is ineffective. When I suffer, I crave an answer as precise as my pain. In what sense is my suffering for the best? And what is the good, if any, to which my suffering will be turned?

God is fair and just, although the final explanation for evil and injustice awaits heaven.[172] I cannot know every purpose for which God permits trouble to come my way, and I would be foolish to give an unequivocal answer to the question, "Why suffering?" Yet my afflictions are not meaningless. They are part of the *specific* good God has determined to do: namely, to turn me to His Word for His discipline and instruction that He may enlighten and deepen me.

The psalmist's argument in Psalm 94 is clear: "How long will the wicked [go unpunished]?" he asks. And God answers: "Does he who *disciplines* nations not punish? Does he who *teaches* man lack knowledge [of their evil]?"[173] God will discipline the ungodly in due time, He insists; but first He must *discipline* and *teach* His own children. A good father begins with his own family.[174]

Affliction, when we accept it with humility, can be instructive, a discipline that leads us to a deeper, fuller life. "Before I was afflicted I went astray," the psalmist says, "but now I obey your word." And again, "It was good for me to be afflicted so that I might learn your decrees." Peter would agree. Affliction, he says, leads us to live no longer for ourselves, but "for the will of God."[175]

Pain, far from being an obstacle to our spiritual growth, can be the condition of it—if we're trained by it. It pushes us closer to God and into His Word. It is the means by which He graciously shapes us to be like His Son, gradually giving us the compassion, contentment, tranquility, and courage we long and pray for. Without pain, God could never make the most of our lives.

> Poets have wronged poor storms: such days are best;
> They purge the air without, within the breast.[176]

That's why Job, who suffered more than anyone I can name, exclaimed in the midst of his troubles, "Blessed is the man whom God corrects," though admittedly, he, like us, found it hard to sustain that thesis at all times.[177]

Are you one whom God has set apart today to instruct through suffering and pain? Endure His discipline patiently. He can make the trial a blessing, using it to draw you into His heart and into His Word, teaching you the lessons He intends you to learn, working in you the grace He means to bestow, giving you "respite from days of trouble."[178] This is the "good" to which your suffering can be turned.[179]

God is making more out of you than you ever thought possible.

> Consider it pure joy, my brothers, whenever you face trials of many kinds, because you know that the testing of your faith develops perseverance.
>
> —James 1:2–3

NOTHING TO LOSE

The delicate seed-globe must break up now—it
gives and gives till it has nothing left.
　　　　—LILIAS TROTTER,
　　　　PARABLES OF THE CROSS

Salsifys grow in delicate profusion in the fields near our place in the mountains of Idaho. From June to August the plants produce spiked yellow flowers that open each morning and go to sleep at noon. In the late summer the flowers close up for good and swell into green pods that burst into puffballs. Then the wind blows the seeds away and there's nothing left but a bare stem.

It strikes me that aging is somewhat like that: Time blows on us, and we lose bits and pieces of ourselves until there's nothing left to lose.

But I'm also reminded that a salsify comes to fruition by surrendering itself. It dies that it might bear much fruit, though it has no idea when or where its seeds will fall. Jesus states the case plainly: "If anyone comes to me and does not hate . . . *his own life*—he cannot be my disciple."[180]

To hate ourselves is not to despise ourselves, but to love and give in such measure that it looks as though we're taking no thought for ourselves, an idea at odds with the wisdom of our age—or of any age for that matter. The fundamental dictum of the human race is to look out for "number one." But Jesus teaches us to give up our lives—forget about them. This is the point of the Beatitudes, the Sermon on the Mount, and most of Jesus' parables. And it is illustrated by His entire life, by the Incarnation, by His willingness to empty himself and, ultimately, to give himself up to death for our sake.

We *find* ourselves by giving ourselves away. "Whoever loses his life for me and for the gospel will save it," Jesus assures us.[181] And Paul, writing of Jesus' willingness to empty himself of self, concludes, "Therefore God exalted him to the highest place."[182]

This is the way to joy, to meaning and purpose, to peace of mind, to tranquility and rest. This is deliverance from the dullness, dreariness, and emptiness of a self-centered existence, deliverance from the vague unhappiness and restlessness that overwhelm us when we live solely for ourselves.

Furthermore, this is the way to sustain the greatest influence on others. "All who would . . . multiply [God's] kingdom must do so through surrender and sacrifice," says Elisabeth Elliot.[183] And in my own experience, those who have had the greatest impact on me are not the brightest and the best but those who have given themselves in love, self-surrender, and sacrifice. These are the men and women who have imparted new life to me.

Lilias Trotter, in her book *Parables of the Cross*, painted a watercolor of a dandelion seed-globe that "long ago surrendered its golden petals, and has reached its crowning stage of dying." Over the top of the dandelion seed-globe she wrote, "I am now ready to be offered." She was quoting Paul: "For I am now ready to be offered," or literally, "I am already being poured out like a drink offering."[184] The drink offering was a goblet of wine poured on the altar of sacrifice. Poof! A flash of luminous flame, and nothing is left but sweet aroma.

Miss Trotter continued: "[The dandelion] stands ready, holding up its little life, not knowing when or where or how the wind that bloweth where it listeth may carry it away. It holds itself no longer for its own keeping, only as something to be given"

> Measure thy life by loss and not by gain,
> Not by the wine drunk, but by the wine poured
>   forth,
> For love's strength standeth in love's sacrifice,
> And he who suffers most has most to give.[185]

SEIZE THE DAY!

"Since life fleets, all is change; the Past gone, seize to-day!"
    —ROBERT BROWNING, "RABBI BEN EZRA"

Light is sweet," the writer of Ecclesiastes says, "and it pleases the eyes to see the sun. However many years a man may live, let him enjoy them all."[186] But remember, the chilly winter of age and infirmity is coming, when . . .

- "the keepers of the house tremble, and the strong men stoop"—our hands begin to tremble and our legs become bent and weak;
- "the grinders cease because they are few, and those looking through the windows grow dim"—our teeth fall out and our eyesight fails;
- "the doors to the street are closed and the sound of grinding fades"—our hearing fails until we can hear almost nothing at all;[187]
- "men rise up at the sound of birds, but all their

songs grow faint"—we don't sleep well at night and wake up with the birds, although, ironically, we can't hear them;

- "men are afraid of heights and of dangers in the streets"—we lose our sense of balance and become afraid of heights and other dangers;
- "the almond tree blossoms and the grasshopper drags himself along and desire no longer is stirred[188]—our hair turns white and falls out; we walk slowly and painfully;
- *then* we go to our eternal home and mourners go about the streets.[189]

If aging doesn't take us, accidental death is always a possibility, when . . .

- "the silver cord is severed"—the spine is broken;
- "the golden bowl is broken"—the skull is fractured;
- "the pitcher is shattered at the spring"—the heart fails;
- "the wheel is broken at the well"—we bleed to death.[190]

Jeremy Taylor, a seventeenth-century Anglican bishop, describes the aging process this way: "At the end of seven years our teeth fall and die before us." This childhood event, he declares, is the first intimation of our mortality, and, the Tooth Fairy notwithstanding, a "formal prologue to [death]."[191]

Taylor then works his way through other intimations of death as age "takes our bodies in pieces, weakening some parts and loosing others." We "taste the grave" as first those parts "that served for ornament" and then those "that served for necessity become useless." Baldness, he claims, is more than a blow to male vanity; it is "but a dressing to our funerals, the proper ornament of mourning."

He continues: "Gray hairs, rotten teeth, dim eyes, trembling joints, short breath, stiff limbs, wrinkled skin, short memory" are all reminders of impending death. Thus God "makes us see death everywhere . . . the expectation of every single person."

So the wise writer of Ecclesiastes counsels us: Enjoy life while you're young, but remember God, for if you forget Him, you'll find no pleasure in your latter days. God is necessary if you want to enjoy *good* old age.

So, I must fear Him *now*—give Him my worship, love, and devotion—and follow Him in obedience "for this is the whole duty of man," or, to quote the wise man precisely, "This is all there is to man."

We were put here on earth to know God and for no other reason. If we do not know Him, no matter what else we have done, our lives are a failure. Thus, barrister William Law concludes, "If you have not chosen God, it will make no difference in the end what you have chosen, for you will have missed the purpose for which you were formed and you will have forsaken the only thing that satisfies."

No matter what our age, this is timely counsel, for if I have grown old and have forgotten God, I will have failed at life no matter what I have accomplished or acquired. I will have missed the purpose for which I was made.

Isn't it good to know that it is never too late to begin again—to put God back into your life?

> Lord, what I once had done with youthful might,
> Had I been from the first true to the truth,
> Grant me, now old, to do—with better sight,
> And humbler heart, if not the brain of youth;
> So wilt thou, in thy gentleness and ruth [pity],
> Lead back thy old soul, by the path of pain
> Round to his best—young eyes and heart and
> brain.[192]

SING A SONG

We follow in His footsteps;
*   What if our feet be torn?*
Where He has marked the pathway
*   All hail the briar and thorn!*
Scarce seen, scarce heard, unreckoned,
*   Despised, defamed, unknown,*
Or heard but by our singing,
*   On, children! ever on!*

—GERHARDT TER STEEGEN

Our home in Boise backs up to a wooded park where I walk most days. An elderly woman walks there at the same time as I. She walks clockwise, I walk counter-clockwise, which means that we meet twice on each lap.

The woman is elderly, tiny, and brown as a betel nut. She has the most lovely, crinkly eyes and wrinkled face that wrinkles even more when she smiles. When she smiles, her whole face lights up!

She has Alzheimer's.

The first time we meet she asks me, "Have I sung my song to you?" I say, "No ma'am." And she sings a children's song to the sun: "Good morning, Mr. Sunshine . . ."

Then she smiles, raises her hand as though rendering a benediction, and moves on.

So we go our separate ways—180 degrees around the circle—until we meet again. She asks: "Have I sung my song?" I say, "Sing it again!" And she does.

I must say, her voice is not very good and she's generally off-key, but no matter. She sings with the enthusiasm of an on-stage diva.

And she is indefatigable! I have seen children mock her and others brush her off in self-preoccupation and embarrassment, but nothing deters her. She smiles sweetly, raises her hand in blessing, and moves on.

Her song haunts me. I can't get it out of my mind. I find myself singing and humming it throughout the day: "Good morning, Mr. Sunshine . . ."

This dear, sweet woman has become a parable and a prayer for me. I, like her, want to make my way along the pathway of life, even when that pathway may be difficult, singing of the Sun of Righteousness who has risen with healing in His wings.[193] And I want to leave behind a lingering melody and memory of His love.

May a new song of God's Son and His salvation be on *my* heart and lips all through this day, and may many hear and put their trust in the Lord.[194]

Barb thou my words with light, make my song
   new,
And men will hear, or when I sing or preach.[195]

A Painful Grace

But as grace operates, it cannot (save through a miracle of that same grace) be other than painful.
—FRANCOIS FÉNELON

Compassion is rare in this world; few seem to know how to respond to others' pain. We share our heartache and draw blank looks from the listener, who then begins to tell his or her story. Later, when we see those to whom we've opened our heart, they seem to have forgotten the matter that troubled us. When that happens, I think, "Perhaps he's not yet suffered enough," for suffering is the means by which we grow more compassionate and merciful toward others who are in distress.

I had the privilege of knowing one of God's most endearing saints, Dr. Oswald Sanders. On one occasion I heard him tell of a meeting at which he spoke, after which, as he was walking off-stage, he overheard one woman whisper to another, "He'll do better when he's suffered a little." So it is with all of us.

C. S. Lewis, in his Narnia chronicle, *The Horse and His Boy*, tells the story of a Calormen noblewoman, Aravis, and her conversion from arrogance and selfishness to humble and compassionate love.

The story begins with Aravis's escape to Narnia and the North to avoid an arranged marriage to Ahoshta Tarkaan, a repulsive, elderly tyrant. To flee, she drugs a servant girl who is in league with her wicked stepmother.

"And what happened to the girl—the one you drugged?" Shasta, her companion (the "Boy"), asks when he hears her story.

"Doubtless she was beaten for sleeping late," said Aravis coolly. "But she was a tool and spy of my stepmother's. I am very glad they should beat her."

"I say, that was hardly fair," Shasta responds in reaction to her indifference to human suffering.

Is it good to be glad that another human being suffers harm, even when they have harmed us? Should we be happy about it? No, because it's always wrong to repay evil for evil: "Do not repay evil with evil or insult with insult, but with blessing," the apostle Peter reminds us, "because to this you were called so that you may inherit a blessing."[196]

In Aravis's case, Aslan himself must teach her that indifference to human suffering is wrong.

In the story, a great lion attacked Aravis outside the gates of Anvard and "jabbed at Aravis with its right paw. Shasta could see all the terrible claws extended.

Aravis screamed and reeled in the saddle. The lion was tearing her shoulders." Shasta was able to rescue her by driving away the beast, but Aravis's wounds were deep and painful and required much time to heal.

Much later, when Aravis and Shasta reached Narnia, Aslan called the young princess to him: "Draw near, Aravis my daughter. See! My paws are velveted. You will not be torn this time."

"This time, sir?" said Aravis.

"It was I who wounded you," said Aslan. "I am the only lion you met in all your journeyings. Do you know why I tore you?

"No, sir."

"The scratches on your back, tear for tear, throb for throb, blood for blood, were equal to the stripes laid on the back of your stepmother's slave because of the drugged sleep you cast upon her. You needed to know what it felt like."

It's always wrong to take pleasure in another person's pain, even when that person has wronged us deeply. Aslan does not argue his case; he simply shows Aravis that her gloating is wrong. Now she *knows* what her servant girl felt like, for she herself has felt great pain.

This is a picture of the mercy of God: In His love He allows us to experience profound suffering so that we may grow in humility, tenderness, and mercy. Our pain, however severe, is a means of grace. It is meant to make us kinder, more compassionate children.

Pressing On

*If I do not experience something far worse than I
yet have done, I shall say the trouble is all in getting started.*

—MRS. GEORGE (TAMSEN E.) DONNER,
MEMBER OF THE ILL-FATED DONNER PARTY,[197]
IN A LETTER DATED JUNE 16, 1846

E very age has its perils, but the greatest peril may
be in thinking that the trouble "is all in getting
started." Sometimes the greatest hazards lie ahead.

Noah, Moses, Gideon, Samuel, David, Solomon,
Uzziah, and a host of biblical people fell into failure
near the end of their days. As the apostle Paul reminds us, "If you think you are standing firm, be
careful that you don't fall!"[198]

"The long, dull, monotonous years of middle-aged
prosperity or middle-aged adversity are excellent cam-
paigning weather for the devil," C. S. Lewis wrote.[199]
And the devil's finest stratagem is sloth, "that great,
sprawling, slug-a-bed sin," as Dorothy Sayers termed it.

Sloth is a spiritual indifference or apathy that has many causes, but may grow out of the belief that we've arrived and have no more ground to gain. Or, that we have little left to give. "Apathy causes one to fall into a deep sleep," the Wise Man said, and then added, "that soul will go hungry."[200] Ah, there it is: a spiritual torpor that starves our souls. Slow down, we say to ourselves; you've given much. Isn't it time to refrain from further sacrifice? Spare yourself. Why go on reading, studying, pursuing God. Stop this strenuous following after.

No! I say. That is not true. We can never stop growing toward God. Holiness is a dynamic thing, a matter of motion. There is no static balance in the spiritual life. We're either moving toward God or away from Him.

St. Gregory put it simply: "When the soul does not direct its efforts to higher things . . . it stoops to concern itself with low desires."[201] When we fail to direct our passions toward heavenly things, we fall into ungodly desires. Bitter animosities demean us; irritability, petulance, impatience, and loss of temper degrade our souls.

So we must never let up, for our adversary does not. He is working every moment to plague and blight our final years. We must pursue God and His righteousness with hearty energy to the end of our days. This was Paul's driving compulsion: "To know Christ and the power of his resurrection and the fellowship of sharing in his sufferings, becoming like him in his death."[202] It must be ours as well.

To know Jesus, to experience more of his life-giving power, to patiently bear our portion of His humiliation and suffering, to become like Him in self-sacrificing love—this is the work that must keep us busy to the end of our days.

We'll not "achieve" the righteousness we seek in this life—that awaits heaven—but you and I must "*press on* to take hold of that for which Christ Jesus took hold of [us]."[203]

So, we must pursue the Lord and His righteousness with all our heart, soul, and mind—with a fierce, unyielding resolve for as many days as He may give us. We must spend time in His presence and choose to do His will. Thus He will fill us with His Spirit and deliver us from the perils that lie ahead.

> But he who would be born again indeed,
> Must wake his soul unnumbered times a day,
> And urge himself to life with holy greed. . .
> Submiss and ready to the making will,
> Athirst and empty, for God's breath to fill.[204]
>   —George MacDonald

REJECTED

To seem the stranger lies my lot, my life
Among strangers. Father and Mother dear,
Brothers and sisters are in Christ not near
And he my peace my parting, sword and strife.
—GERARD MANLEY HOPKINS

So now you're old and unwanted—secondhand, surplus, unasked for. It's easy to retreat into self-pity and think bad thoughts about yourself.

Many seniors do. They live with unexpressed depression that grows through the years because they feel cast off and uncared for. Disappointments mount as colleagues, friends, and family, involved in their own lives, families, activities, and interests, forget we're still around. No visits, no phone calls, no e-mails, no cards.

Our Lord understands. He was despised and rejected—"looked down on and passed over."[205] And His rejection, like ours, caused Him deep sorrow, for He was fully human (though fully God) and felt the entire range of human emotions, and thus is acquainted with our grief. But He knew what to do with rejection, as is revealed in a story that He told.

On one occasion, when Israel's leaders sought to kill Jesus, He spoke of a vineyard owner who sent his son to deal with some unruly workers. The workers rejected the son, killed him, and threw his body away. But the owner of the vineyard had the last word, said Jesus, because "'The stone the builders rejected has become the capstone; the Lord has done this, and it is marvelous in our eyes.'"[206]

Jesus was quoting a psalm[207] that is oft-quoted in the New Testament, and was foretelling His own rejection, suffering, and distress, as well as His future vindication.

Who was the stone? Jesus. Who were the builders? The power-elite of Jesus' day, who mocked Him and rejected His love. How did the stone become the capstone? God placed it there through the resurrection in which He raised His Son out of this world and its abuse and placed Him on high.

This, then, was Jesus' confidence: that He, though hated and rejected, scorned and crucified here on earth would eventually, eternally, be exalted to the right hand of His Father far above all betrayal and denial. This was His "marvelous" vindication.

This is our vindication as well. Someday we, too, will be raised out of our ungrateful world and given a home where we will be sheltered from all abuse by our

Father's love. All this is done because, as the psalmist reminds us again and again, "God's love endures *forever*." We are loved *now*, but as yet we know little of our inheritance. Someday we will be welcomed into our Father's house and will be loved beyond all imagination *forever and ever*! Is this not the infinite affection for which we have longed throughout our lives?

So this day we may say with the psalmist and with Jesus, "The Lord is with me; I will not be afraid. What can man do to me?"[208]

I read somewhere that G. Campbell Morgan, who was known as "the prince of expositors" in the early twentieth century, at first failed his examinations for the Wesleyan pulpit. In deep disappointment he sent a one-word telegram to his father: "Rejected." His father wrote back: "Rejected on earth; accepted in heaven."

So it will *always* be.

THE YOKE

Who best bear his mild yoke, they serve him best.
—JOHN MILTON, "ON HIS BLINDNESS"

There was an occasion on which Judah's king, Zedekiah, and a number of dignitaries from surrounding nations gathered in Jerusalem to plot rebellion against Babylon.[209]

Jeremiah the prophet, who was always unpredictable, crashed the party, bearing a heavy wooden yoke on his shoulders and offering this explanation: "'Bow your neck under the yoke of the king of Babylon; serve him and his people, and you will live.'"[210]

History proved him right. Those who patiently endured Babylon's yoke lived in Jerusalem in peace and safety; those who resisted lost their lives.[211]

Jeremiah elsewhere said of his own transgressions: "'My sins have been bound into a yoke; by his hands they were woven together. They have come upon my neck and the Lord has sapped my strength. He has handed me over to those I cannot withstand.'"[212]

173

I think of those who have sinned recklessly in their youth and who now must bear the consequences—an alienated family, a ruined reputation, a sexually transmitted disease. Although the sin itself, if confessed and repented of, has been fully forgiven, the sad consequences of sins may linger on and on.

Have your sins been bound into a yoke that causes great grief? If so, "bow your neck under the yoke" and bear it patiently. Let God determine the time and the terms of the burden you bear and rely on His mercy, remembering that all things, even the dire consequences of your sins, flow out of His wisdom and love.[213]

The yoke may cause great grief, but resistance only leads to greater discomfort. We must endure the hardship of discipline.[214] We must learn the lessons of faith and patience that are found in the burden. This, and not escape, leads to "an eternal glory that far outweighs them all."[215]

God is not punitive. He disciplines us "for our good, that we may share in his holiness."[216] Pain and sorrow become the means by which He frees us from our preoccupation with earthly things and turns our hearts to unseen, eternal realities. He searches into our character and reveals its flaws so that His likeness may grow within us. And thus we come to the end of ourselves that we may share His glory.

Though chastened, we'll not be overwhelmed; though corrected and diminished, God will not "fin-

ish [us] off," for He has "more work left to do" on us.[217]
And in His time, when His holy work is done, He will
lift the burden from our shoulders—in this world or
in the next.

In the meantime, we must pray for those we've
damaged by our sin, knowing that God can bring good
even from the suffering we've inflicted on others.

Finally, we must not grow anxious about those
whom God is using to chafe us. They may go beyond
His boundaries, as Nebuchadnezzar did, but their
time will come.[218] There's no need to quarrel or con-
tend with them, or to take their judgment into our
hands. We must leave them to God, the judge of all,
and be at peace.

> He will judge the world in righteousness
> and the peoples in his truth.[219]

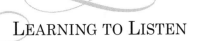

LEARNING TO LISTEN

A wise old owl sat in an oak,
The more he heard, the less he spoke;
The less he spoke, the more he heard;
Why aren't we all like that wise old bird?

Renè Descarte, the sixteenth-century philosopher, said, "I think, therefore I am." Sarah, our granddaughter, says, "You are, therefore I talk." Silence has never been golden to Sarah.

Some years ago I was sitting in our family room trying to read a *Time* magazine while, at the same time, Sarah was trying to carry on a conversation with me. To my shame I was paying little attention, responding to her comments with an occasional grunt.

Finally in exasperation she crawled into my lap and got in my face. "Papa," she shouted, "are you listening to me?"

"Sarah," I confessed, putting down my magazine,

"I haven't been listening well. Forgive me. I'll listen to you now."

My commitment to Sarah is one that I want to keep on other occasions as well. It's one of the gifts "of what remains"[220] that I can give to others—to talk less and listen better. As Frasier Crane would say, "I'm listening"—or, to be more honest, I'm trying to learn how to listen.

I want to listen well so that when I finish a conversation, others will walk away knowing there's at least one person in this care-less world who has some inkling of what they're doing, thinking, and feeling. I want to hear the hushed undertones of their hearts. I want them to know that I care.

Listening, however, doesn't come easy for me. For years I was paid to talk; I was a "word monger" to borrow Augustine's apt description of a teacher. It comes as a revelation to me that I can do more with my ears now than I can with my mouth.

In her book *Listening to Others,* Joyce Huggett relates her experiences of listening to suffering people. She says they often talk about all she's done for them. "On many occasions," she writes, "I have not 'done' anything. I have 'just listened.' I quickly came to the conclusion that 'just listening' was indeed an effective way of helping others."

This was the help Job's wordy, would-be friends failed to give him. They were "miserable comforters," he complained. "'Oh, that I had someone to hear me!'"

Job is not alone in his longing. All human beings want to be heard, and listening is one of the best ways in the world to love others. Listening says, "You matter to me."[221]

Kenneth Grahame's Badger in *The Wind in the Willows* knew how to do it.

> He sat in his arm-chair at the head of the table, and nodded gravely at intervals as the animals told their story; and he did not seem surprised or shocked at anything, and he never said, "I told you so," or, "Just what I always said," or remarked that they ought to have done so-and-so, or ought not to have done something else. The Mole began to feel very friendly towards him.

Listening is a lost art these days. We don't listen well and we aren't used to being listened to. Most of our words simply disappear into the air.

I have a friend who, when he goes to noisy parties and people ask how he's doing, on occasion has replied quietly, "My business went belly-up this week, the bank foreclosed on my house, my wife left me, and I have terminal cancer." "Wonderful!" one man murmured, as he pumped my friend's hand and moved on. I keep wondering if I've done something similar to others.

Some years ago I came across the following advice about listening—which I'm still in the process of learning and applying:

- When I'm thinking about an answer while others are talking—I'm not listening.
- When I give unsolicited advice—I'm not listening. (Unsolicited advice always sounds like criticism.)
- When I suggest they shouldn't feel the way they do—I'm not listening.
- When I apply a quick fix to their problem—I'm not listening.
- When I fail to acknowledge their feelings—I'm not listening.
- When I fidget, glance at my watch, and appear to be rushed—I'm not listening.
- When I fail to maintain eye contact—I'm not listening.
- When I don't ask follow-up questions—I'm not listening.
- When I top their story with a bigger, better story of my own—I'm not listening.
- When they share a difficult experience and I counter with one of my own—I'm not listening.

Listening is hard work, and most of us are unwilling to put in the time—and *time* is the operative word. Listening means setting aside our own timetable and tendency to hurry on to our next destination. It means settling into a relaxed, unhurried, leisurely pace. "Only in the ambiance of leisure," Eugene Peterson writes, "do persons know they are listened to with absolute seriousness, treated with dignity and importance."

In leisure we regard others' interests as more important than ours.[222] In leisure we say, "You are more significant than anything I have to do right now. You are the only one who counts, the one for whom I am willing to forgo my other obligations, appointments, and meetings. I have time for *you*." In leisure, we listen long enough to hear the other person's true heart so that if we do speak, we speak with wisdom.

A leisurely pace, a listening ear, a loving heart. May you and I, by God's grace, acquire them.

THE WORLD'S LAST NIGHT

> *The doctrine of the Second Coming has failed,*
> *so far as we are concerned, if it does not make us*
> *realize that at every moment of every year in our*
> *lives Donne's question "What if this present were*
> *the world's last night?" is equally relevant.*
>
> —C. S. LEWIS[223]

I love to read old newspapers from the days of the Idaho frontier. One such paper is *The Owyhee Avalanche*, a chronicle that covered events in and around Owyhee County (the county to the south of us) in the mid to late nineteenth century.

On May 4, 1867, the paper carried this report: "James Fraser was shot and killed by Indians last Friday evening between sunset and dark." Fraser was a prospector working a gulch below Wagontown in the Owyhee Mountains of Idaho, closing in on pay dirt. He didn't plan to die that day . . . but he did. You just never know.

Death meets us every where . . . and enters in
at many doors. [It enters by the fall of a chariot
and the stumbling at a stone, by a full meal or
an empty stomach, by watching at the wine or by
watching at prayers, by the sun or the moon, by a
heat or a cold, by sleepless nights or sleeping days,
by water frozen into the hardness and sharpness
of a dagger, or water thawed into the floods of a
river, by a hair or a raisin, by violent motion or sitting still, by severity or dissolution, by every thing
in nature and every thing in chance.[224]

The apostle Peter agrees. "The end of all things
is near."[225] This night—tonight—may be "the world's
last night"—at least for me. I may go to God this day,
or He may come for me. This could be the last hour
of my life.

So, I ask myself: How should I invest my time?
What activities and attitudes should fill my final
hours? Is there some magnificent gesture, some grand
and glorious act to mark the end of my days?

First, I must *pray*: "Be clear minded and self-controlled so that you can pray," Peter writes. Prayer is
my access to God, the way I can stay in touch with
Him. It's not so much that prayer moves God, but that
it moves me. It aligns me more closely with what He
is doing, and conforms me to His will.

I must bring sobriety to prayer, Peter says. It's
not that prayer must be joyless, for it can be whimsi-

cal, light-hearted, musical, full of mirth. No, what Peter inveighs against is superficiality. I must take *seriously* my need to fill my days with prayer because that is the secret of a useful, God-filled life—the means by which God can use me for the highest good. Without prayer I will accomplish exactly nothing.

And then I must *love* deeply—with great care and determination, "because love covers over a multitude of sins." Love and forgiveness mark me as God's child and remind others of His love. "No one can see God," John said, but they can see me.

Perhaps I can do nothing for a difficult neighbor, a struggling brother, a suffering friend. But I can love them. A smile, a note, a kind word, a brief touch can be the greatest thing in the world when I offer it in love. And even when my journey leads into illness, weakness, and infirmed old age, my work can be in loving, which in the end will be my greatest gift to God and to others.

In addition, I must *offer hospitality* to others without complaining. I can open my home and my heart to those in need; I can be available to *anyone* who happens to come my way. "Who is my neighbor?" Jesus answers: the next needy person you meet. I must keep my heart open to others and welcome all comers.

Then, I must use whatever gifts God has given me to *serve* others, "faithfully administering God's grace in its various forms." The gifts I have been given and the work I am called to do are from one mind. The

God who made me made my path. For whatever days God gives me, I must put into practice His special design and purpose for me so I may live in loving service to Him and to others.

And finally, I must do all these things "with the strength God provides." God must put into me all that He wants to take out of me. I am nothing; He is everything. To *Him* be the glory (not me).

Prayer, love, hospitality, and humble service. How simple and how satisfying to do these things as though they are the last things I will do on earth. To do them lovingly, faithfully, patiently this day and the next day and the next day . . . If so, the last day will take care of itself.

It's never too late to get started; we're never too old to begin. "I must begin *today*!"[226]

On Yaks

We have been talking about faith ever since the Lord came. It is not exhausted yet, and God forbid that I should think that I know yet what faith is; although I know a little what it is.[227]

—GEORGE MACDONALD

There's a yak," Carolyn said nonchalantly as we sped down the highway last summer. "Yeah, sure," I replied, with more irony in my voice than I intended.

"It *was* a yak!" Carolyn harrumphed. "I SAW IT WITH MY OWN EYES!" Then she lapsed into ominous silence.

"Well, there's one way to settle this matter," I muttered, and turned the car around and drove back to the place where she claimed to have seen the beast.

"There," she pointed, and exclaimed as the animal came into sight, "See? Now do you believe me?"

It was indeed a yak. I was chastened in my unbelief.

This exchange set me to thinking about faith and its properties. Like George MacDonald, I do not think that I know yet what faith is, but I learned a little what it is through that exchange. It occurs to me now that faith means believing *something*. But it is more. Faith is believing *someone*. Let me explain.

Faith, by biblical definition, is "being sure of what we hope for and certain of what we do not see."[228] Faith is unrestricted, unreserved, unconditional certainty. "It is part of the concept of belief itself that a man is *certain* of that in which he believes."[229]

But that conviction is based on "things not seen."[230] Faith's certainty does not rest on empirical, first-hand evidence, but on someone else's observations. When we have seen something for ourselves, we no longer believe; we "know." A "believer," then, in the strictest sense of the word, accepts a matter as real and true on the testimony of someone else.

I know, for example, that there was a yak on the road that day because I saw it with my own eyes. But if Carolyn tells me these days that she has seen another yak, while I may not *know* it, I will *believe* it (the fact of a yak); or, more exactly, I will believe *her,* for she has proved herself to be a credible witness.

Which brings me to the point of this chapter: I believe the stories about Jesus because I believe His apostles, who were eyewitnesses of the things He did and said; I believe that their firsthand reports are true. As the apostle John put it: "That . . . which we have heard, which we have seen with our eyes, which we have looked at and our hands have touched . . . [w]e proclaim to you. . ."[231]

I believe *something* (the words and works of Jesus), but I also believe *someone* (those who were eyewitnesses of Jesus' words and works). John concludes his gospel on this note: "Jesus did many other miraculous signs in the presence of his disciples, which are not recorded in this book. *But these are written that you may believe* that Jesus is the Christ, the Son of God. . ."[232] This is biblical faith: believing what John and the other apostles saw and then said about Jesus.

And therein lies the difficulty, because most of us are from Missouri; you have to *show* us. *Seeing* is believing. Like Thomas, we want to *see* the angry prints of the nails in Jesus' hands; we want to *touch* the terrible wound in His side. We want to see for ourselves.[233] We feel the rebuke of Jesus' words: "Blessed are those who have not seen and yet have believed."[234] And we hear ourselves say, "Lord, I believe; help my unbelief!"[235]

First, let me say that our Lord is not angry with us because we find it hard to believe. He shared our human limitations and struggles when He was made flesh. Jesus himself had moments of uncertainty and doubt and needed His Father's reassurance.[236]

Angry? No. But He does want us to believe, for our faith pleases Him more than anything else we can do. How, then, can we know with complete assurance that what Jesus said and did is true?

By obeying Him. Jesus made this clear: "Whoever has my commands and obeys them, he is the one who loves me. He who loves me will be loved by my Father, and I too will love him and show myself to him." He also said, "My teaching is not my own. It comes from him who sent me. If anyone chooses to do God's will, he will find out whether my teaching comes from God. . ."[237]

How does Jesus show himself to us (make himself real)? How do we *know* that He is real? *By acting on His word.* George MacDonald writes: "I ask you, have you been trying the things not seen? Have you been proving them? This is what God puts in your hands. He says, 'I tell you I Am, you act upon that; for I know that your conscience moves you to it; you act upon that and you will find whether I Am or not, and what I Am.'"[238]

Do you see? Faith in its true sense does not belong to the intellect alone, nor to the intellect first, but to the conscience and to the will. The faithful person says, "I cannot prove that there is a God, but, O God, if you hear me anywhere, help me do your will."

Faith is the turning of the eye to the light; it is the sending of the feet into the path that is required; it is the putting of the hands to the task that the conscience says ought to be done. It is "the proving of things not seen" and of which we cannot, at first, be sure of. It is putting Jesus' words to the test, doing the very thing that you suppose to be the will of God.[239]

So whatever your uncertainties, act upon what Jesus is asking you to do today. Don't wait for assurance. Just *do* it. Has He asked you to love a difficult and demanding child or spouse, to bear patiently with a painful disability, to be brave in the face of harsh criticism and misunderstanding? Do it! "What saves a man is to take a step. Then another step," C. S. Lewis said.

You will not be able to obey perfectly, of course—that is something only One has been able to do. But if you choose the right thing and try to do it, God will give you all the help you need to carry on. Then, in time (I cannot say how or when) you will "see" and you will "know" for yourself. Then, your whole being will be caught up in the sheer delight of loving and being loved by our Lord.

And this is that for which we were made.

FOOL'S GOLD

All that is gold does not glitter.
—J. R. R. TOLKIEN

There was a television show many years ago about an invisible man. He could go anywhere and do anything and no one knew he was there. I have become that man.

I go to check-out counters and perky young clerks look right through me, unaware that a human being stands before them. I sit in discussions with bright young theologians and no one acknowledges my presence or asks if I have an opinion. It's good to remember, on those occasions, Tolkien's wise proverb: "All that is gold does not glitter."

Back in the 1860s a prospector named Captain Tom Morgan filed a claim on a hard-to-find drainage in the mountains northeast of Boise, Idaho, and rode into town claiming he had discovered over $50,000 worth of gold. After a legendary spending spree, his "gold" was discovered to be chemically enhanced iron pyrite—also known as "fool's gold."

Captain Morgan was never caught, nor was he ever seen again, but his skullduggery is memorialized in the name the site bears to this day, Bogus Basin, and proves again that Shakespeare was right: "All that glitters is not gold."

Most of us, at one time or another, have been fooled by those who shimmer and shine, but whose hearts are dark and deceitful. We've learned that outward beauty can be a façade, an affectation that conceals evil, self-serving motives. Be wary of those who look too good to be true, for too often they are.

J. R. R. Tolkien, however, turns the proverb upside down and finds an equal and opposite truth: "All that is gold does not glitter." In other words, as ugliness can be cloaked in beauty, so beauty can be hidden in an off-putting presence.

Early in the story of *The Lord of the Rings*, the hobbit Frodo and his halfling friends have arrived at the village of Bree and have taken a room at the inn of The Prancing Pony. Riders had come from the south the day before—strange, suspicious-looking men who are also lodged at the inn. But the strangest of all is a tall dark man who sits in a shadowy corner, wrapped in a cloak with a hood that hides his face.

He is a Ranger, the innkeeper Mr. Butterbur says, a solitary wanderer who comes and goes at will and whose business is shrouded in mystery. His presence is grim and forbidding.

Then Butterbur remembers that three months earlier the wizard Gandalf had left a letter with him that he was supposed to deliver to Mr. Frodo Baggins. In the letter Gandalf writes: "You may meet a friend of mine on the Road: a Man, lean, dark, tall, by some called Strider. He knows our business and will help you."

In a postscript to the letter, Gandalf offers this warning, information, and prophecy:

> All that is gold does not glitter,
>> Not all those who wander are lost;
> The old that is strong does not wither,
>> Deep roots are not reached by the frost.
> From the ashes a fire shall be woken,
>> A light from the shadows shall spring;
> Renewed shall be blade that was broken;
>> The crownless again shall be king.[240]

Who could have guessed that the dark rider is, in fact, Aragorn, son of Arathorn, a "crownless" king, an ancient warrior with deep wisdom who will become a fast friend, faithful guide, and guardian to Frodo and his friends—which, of course, is Tolkien's point: an unappealing presence can conceal a heart of gold. We're fools not to know it.

The media and other elements of our culture have

taught folks to court the buff, the best-dressed, and the beautiful and attribute worth to them. The dull, the dowdy, the homely, the elderly are discounted.

But wisdom teaches otherwise: "The LORD does not look at the things man looks at. Man looks at the outward appearance, but the LORD looks at the heart."[241] Wisdom leads us to go beyond appearance and look within our souls for virtue and the beauty of holiness, for authentic worth lies just there.

Remember our Lord: "He had no beauty or majesty to attract us to him, nothing in his appearance that we should desire him. He was despised . . . and we esteemed him not."[242] Yet His heart was pure gold.

Our Lord is building into *us* pure gold, silver, and precious stones, and what matters in the end is not what has happened to the outer person, but what's going on inside. We may be nothing much to look at—no glitter or glamour— but our souls can shimmer and shine. On that basis, and that basis alone, we must assign value to ourselves.

But then, having written all that, I have to ask myself, "On what basis do I evaluate *others?* What kind of fool am I?"[243]

THINGS I CAN'T DO ANY LONGER

You are no longer equal to the tasks which once
you undertook with ease. The eye may be dim,
the ear dull, the breath short, the heart faint, the
hand unsteady, and the golden bowl of life almost
broken. And because these things are in contrast
with the long day of usefulness which you once
enjoyed, you are inclined to be despondent; you
feel that you are a burden to others, and that you
are in their way.

—HENRY DURBANVILLE,
THE BEST IS YET TO BE

Carolyn will tell you that I'm an impossibly opti-
mistic person who rarely sees the difficulties in
life that others see. I awaken most mornings full of
lively enthusiasm, an attitude reminiscent of *Mad*
magazine's mascot, Alfred E. Neuman: "What, me
worry?"

Lately, however, when I allow my thoughts to
dwell on the fact that I'm well past prime, I find my-

self somewhat deflated. Yet these pensive moments can be good for the heart, because they make me think long and earnestly about my motives, intentions, enthusiasms, and real interests.[244]

My melancholy, as I'm beginning to understand it, comes mostly from losses and consequent disappointment, from the realization that certain activities I've always enjoyed must now be curtailed. There are some things—activities from which I formerly derived great satisfaction—that I can no longer enjoy. They're much too difficult for an older man to do. I'm no longer equal to the tasks that once I undertook with ease.

Such brooding only leads to deeper discouragement, however. So I'm learning to ask myself, "Can I be content with these losses, knowing that losses are part of aging and as such are the will of God?"

Dr. Robert Horton, a Bible scholar and teacher, who, in the zenith of his career, could hold congregations spellbound by his eloquence, in his last years struggled from the feeling that he had been set aside. Churches no longer wanted his services, publishers no longer sought his manuscripts, people didn't ask for his counsel.

"A man discovers one day that his mind has lost its old elasticity," he wrote, "that it is no longer equal to the tasks laid upon it; and that those who came after him are being preferred before him. Fretful impatience cannot alter the facts, although it may murder his own peace of mind. *Let him accept them as the will of God for him; then all the bitterness goes.*"[245]

So, with this encouragement I say to myself, "If I accept my lot with a quiet patience, not chafing against it, I will find that it's not without its compensations." Indeed, "in acceptance lieth peace."[246]

God's will is a soft pillow for my head and a place of peace and comfort for my heart.

Thou sweet beloved will of God,
My anchor ground, my fortress hill,
My spirit's silent, fair abode,
In Thee I hide me, and am still.

Within this place of certain good,
Love evermore expands her wings,
Or nestling in Thy perfect choice,
Abides content with what it brings.

O lightest burden, sweetest yoke,
It lifts, it bears my happy soul,
It giveth wings to this poor heart;
My freedom is Thy grand control.

Upon God's will I lay me down,
As child upon its mother's breast;
No silken couch, nor softest bed,
Could ever give me such deep rest.

Thy wonderful, grand will, my God,
With triumph now I make it mine;
And faith shall cry a joyous 'Yes'
To every dear command of Thine.

—Madam Guyon

THE WORK OF OUR HANDS

Life is a vapor, but that is long enough to do the right thing.

—RICHARD SWENSON

A few years ago Carolyn and I were vacationing in a friend's condo on the Oregon coast. One morning I got up early to take a walk on the beach, access to which was gained by a winding path through thick bushes that overarched and completely enclosed it. The bushes hadn't been trimmed in some time, and they were crowding into the path making it difficult in some places to push through. Even with daylight it was a dark and gloomy place.

At the bottom of the walk there was a gate that was locked to prevent access to the condo from the beach. As I got out my key to unlock the gate, I heard a noise behind me and turned to face a large, bearded unkempt, sinister-looking man bearing down on me through the bushes. He had a sickle in his hand.

I've been told that your entire life passes through

198

your mind at the moment of death, but the only thought that went through my mind was that I had just bought the farm.

As it turned out, however, my "assailant" was merely the gardener making his way down the path to trim the bushes. He was a rather pleasant fellow, and after I realized that he didn't intend to murder me, we had an amiable chat.

As I moved through the gate and out onto the beach, I began to think about the tenuous nature of life. I've already used up most of my allotted time— exceeded my three-score and ten. Life is too uncertain, too fragile, to treat it carelessly. So I frequently ask myself, "Have I left anything behind of significance? Will there be any enduring evidence that I've been here?"

Augustine said, "Do you wish to be great? Then begin by *being*." Enduring greatness stems from what we *are*, not from what we do. Though we may seem to be doing nothing worthwhile, we can be doing everything worthwhile if our lives are being styled by God's wonderful grace. Set aside through sickness or seclusion, we can still be productive. Bedridden or housebound, our holiness can still bear fruit. "Being" is what matters.

The other lasting thing we can do is to touch as many people as possible with God's love through the kindness and compassion we show. "Even in darkness light dawns for the upright, for the gracious and compassionate and righteous man . . . a righteous man will be remembered forever."[247]

"We are immortal until our work on earth is done," said George Whitefield. I often think of that maxim when I see a friend languishing, bedridden and helpless, burdened with an active mind in a useless body. "Why doesn't God take him home?" I ask.

I'm reminded then that the time of our death is not determined by anyone or anything here on earth—not physicians, not actuarial tables, not the average life span of a human being. That decision is made in the councils of heaven. When we have done all God has in mind for us to do, then and only then will He take us home. As Paul put it, "When David had served God's purpose in his own generation, he fell asleep"—and not one moment before.[248]

In the meantime, until God takes us home, there's plenty to do. "As long as it is day, we must do the work of him who sent me," Jesus said. "Night is coming, when no one can work."[249] Night is coming when we will close our eyes on this world, or our Lord will bring this world to a close. Each day brings one of those two conclusions a little bit closer.

As long as we have the light of day, we must work—not to conquer, acquire, accumulate, and retire, but to make visible the invisible Christ and to touch men and women, boys and girls with His love. If we have done these things, we will have done all we can do and we can rest easy. No matter what else we've done or have not done, we will not have labored in vain.

So "let us run with perseverance the race marked out for us."[250]

> While there is still time, while we are still in the body and are able to fulfill all these things by the light of this life, we must hasten to do now what will profit us for eternity.
>
> —St. Benedict

READINESS

If you know the enemy and know yourself, the victory is not at risk.

SUN TZU, *THE ART OF WAR* (C. 400 B.C.)

Our son Randy, whose business it is to know such things, told me about the OODA Loop the other day.

The OODA Loop comes from Colonel John Boyd and his concept of decision-making in battlefield conditions. OODA is an acronym for Observe, Orient, Decide, and Act. In its simplest form it describes the process by which combatants react to an enemy threat: (1) they observe the threat as it occurs; (2) they orient themselves to the threat; (3) they decide what action they will take; and (4) they act. All of which takes a certain amount of time.

Boyd's theory claims that the key to success in an encounter is to shorten a combatant's reaction time by *formulating a strategy ahead of time* for dealing with specific threats. In other words, one thinks through the Loop before an encounter.

Success, therefore, depends on mental preparation: anticipating every strategy an opponent might use and *deciding in advance what one's response will be* so that when an attack occurs the appropriate action becomes instinctual and automatic.

This theory has an elegant simplicity that lends itself to many applications, not the least of which is our ongoing conflict with evil—within and without. It offers what the wise person needs, according to Proverbs: guidance for waging war and wise counsel for victory.[251]

It seems to me that Peter had something like Boyd's premise in mind when he enjoined us to "be self-controlled [think it through] and alert [in readiness], [for] your enemy the devil prowls around like a roaring lion looking for someone to devour."[252] In other words, we must be mentally prepared and know what to do when under attack.

This readiness is what early Christians called *solertia*, a Latin word that means a process of deliberation by which an individual envisions an impending circumstance and prepares for it by deciding beforehand what she or he will do. Thus, when the crisis arrives the person is not driven by emotion and passion, but by calm, reasoned resolution.[253] This is *providentia* (another word the early Christians used) or "seeing before"—envisioning what needs to be done before one has to do it and giving thought to what has to be done and how to do it.

Solertia means, among other things, taking time each morning to think through the day and anticipate difficult and dangerous situations so that our response to spiritual threats is immediate and instinctual. (Do I have a meeting with someone "unfriendly" today? What do I think he or she will say? How can I respond in truth and love? Am I facing sexual temptation for which I must be forearmed? What steps must I take to guard my thoughts and actions? Do I anticipate a challenge in my business in which I'll be tempted to bargain away my integrity? What will I do if I am told to lie and my job is on the line?) Having deliberated in advance, I can respond to moral crises with calm conviction, for the decision has already been made.

It's not mere forethought that saves us, however. Jesus instructs us to "watch and pray" lest we fall into temptation, for we may be willing and resolute, but the flesh (our unaided humanity) is weak.[254] It's not by decision and determination alone, but by prayer—utter dependence on God—that we prevail.

> Before you go forth of your closet, after your prayers are done, sit yourself down a little while, and consider what you are to do that day, what matter of business is like to employ you, or to tempt you; and take particular resolution against

that, whether it be matter of wrangling, or anger, or covetousness, or vain courtship, or feasting: and when you enter upon it, remember, upon what you resolved in your closet. If you are likely to have nothing extraordinary that day, a general recommendation of the affairs of that day to God in your prayers will be sufficient; but if there be any thing foreseen that is not usual, *be sure to be armed for it, by a hearty, though a short prayer*, and an earnest, prudent resolution beforehand: and then watch when the thing comes.[255]

Jesus said to His disciples: "Things that cause people to sin are bound to come . . . So watch yourselves."[256]

AUTUMN COLORS

Nature is ever singing to a child a more exquisite song, and telling a more wonderful tale.
—WILLIAM WORDSWORTH

I notice more things these days. This year it's the colors of autumn. Why, I ask myself, do trees turn into this collage of radiant maroon, red, orange, and yellow?

There's a perfectly natural explanation, of course. Trees are shades of green in the summer because chlorophyll, a green pigment in the leaves, absorbs red and blue light from the sun. The light reflected from the leaves, diminished in red and blue, appears green to our eyes.

Chlorophyll is an unstable substance, and bright sunlight causes it to decompose rapidly so plants must continuously synthesize and regenerate it. The shortening days and cool nights of autumn, however, interfere with this process, and as chlorophyll breaks down, the green colors of the leaves begin to fade.

The leaves of some trees—birches and "quakies" (aspens) for example—contain carotene, a yellow pigment, and thus change from green to bright yellow as the chlorophyll degrades. In other trees the action of sugar in the leaves creates anthocyanin, a red pigment, causing the yellowing leaves to turn maroon, purple, and bright red as the chlorophyll fades.

As I said before, there's a perfectly natural explanation.

But, I ask you, why all this just for *color*? Color serves no practical purpose, at least none that scientists have been able to discover. And why are there photoreceptors in our eyes that enable us to see it? Who can explain this?

John Calvin, that's who: "If it be asked what cause induced [God] to create all things at first, and now inclines him to preserve them, we shall find that there could be no other cause than his own goodness."[257]

No other cause than God's goodness? Indeed. Goodness is the point of all creation. God created and colored the world and exuded over what He had made: "Ah, that's beautiful!"[258] He exclaimed. "My children will love it!"

I would never for a moment denigrate the labors and discoveries of scientists, but their explanations are never enough, for they cannot tell us *why* things *ultimately* exist—that is, for what purpose.[259] For that insight we need revelation and disclosure, not discovery.

It is through God's Word, not scientific analysis, that we enter into nature's deepest secrets and understand God's "why." There "we understand in a moment things that no man of science, prosecuting his investigations from the surface with all the aids that keenest human intellect can supply, would reach in the longest lifetime."[260] There we understand that God is love and made the whole world for our good!

Dante, in the very last line of his *Divine Comedy,* sums up his argument on the mystery of God's eternal affection by stating that his love for us is the motive and the means "whereby the sun doth move /And all the stars."

Why, then, autumn colors? Our heavenly Father does it on purpose to make the world more beautiful for our childlike delight—and for no other reason.

He's like that, you know.

Nothing Left to Prove

A few fortunate individuals never seem to struggle with self-esteem. I remember hearing an interview with the great Hall of Fame quarterback Roger Staubach on ESPN some years ago in which he was asked about his early athletic career. He said that when he played Little League baseball as a boy, in tense bases-loaded, one-run-ahead situations, he would say to himself, "Hit the ball to me! Hit it to me."

When I was a kid playing baseball, I was always praying under my breath: "Please don't hit the ball to me! Please don't hit the ball to me! Hit it to anyone but me." Many of you can probably identify with that point of view.

One way the world tries to deal with lack of self-esteem is to suggest that we itemize our assets and liabilities. That's not entirely wrong. It's good to be objective about oneself. Paul says, "Do not think of yourself more highly than you ought, but rather *think of yourself with sober judgment.*"[261] In other words, we need to know who we are.

Obviously, I shouldn't feel bad about myself because I'm not playing quarterback for the Dallas Cowboys. God has not gifted me to play that role. But there are things I can do and can do reasonably well. So it's a good exercise from time to time to remind ourselves that we are gifted in certain ways and that all of us have something of significance to give to the world and to the church.

Another secular solution to self-esteem is to do something about your liabilities: Go back to school. Join a gym and get in shape. Buy clothes. Create "a new you"—more self-assured version of yourself.

Again, there's nothing wrong with trying to make the most of what we have. But if we're not careful, the whole exercise will degenerate into narcissism and constant attention to our own bodies, muscles, or clothing. And when all the objectifying and re-doing is over, most of us will still have that one anguish: low self-esteem.

There's only one way to deal with that issue: We must learn to see ourselves as God sees us and know that He highly values us.

In the stock market there is a concept called "value transfer." Certain stocks take on value because credible brokers believe in them. That principle operates in almost every realm of life: A thing is given worth when valuable people ascribe value to it.

Suppose, for example, you're a fledgling artist exhibiting your first efforts at Arts in the Park. No one is interested in your work. Those who do stop gaze for a moment and then look bored and move on. But then, along comes Rembrandt, the great Dutch painter—the master of light and shadow. He stops to peruse your paintings. "Pure genius!" he exclaims. "Marvelous talent! Great potential. I'll give you a million dollars (guilders?) for this work!"

God feels the same way about you. You are of infinite worth in His eyes. Imagine! The Creator of the universe thinks you're someone very special, even if you're very old. It's been said that "faith is the courage to accept acceptance." How can I not value what God values?

I think of Bow Wow. Thirty years ago one of our sons adopted a rag dog he called Bow Wow. Bow Wow was the most precious thing that boy possessed. He had toys with more intrinsic value, but none did he love or value more. Bow Wow was Linus's blanket, Radar's teddy bear, the Velveteen Rabbit—all rolled up in one. Bow Wow got dragged everywhere, and in time became incredibly dirty and ragged. But my, how he was loved!

We are God's rag dogs—precious beyond all measure because we are loved by the One who is Love itself.

It's that perspective that enables us to be chivalrous and magnanimous to others. Once we understand how deeply we're loved, we don't need to win all the time. We can set aside our envy and jealousy; we don't have to put others down or score a string of petty victories to feel good about ourselves. We don't have to prove anything. We have nothing left to prove. We're loved by Infinite Love.

The Highways to Zion

This world is not my home;
I'm just a-passin' through.
— SPIRITUAL

Blessed are those . . . who have set their hearts on pilgrimage," writes the psalmist.[262] I'm fond of that verse, 'cause I'm a traveling man, drawn by a picnicker's hankering for "a better place," and I suspect you may be too.

We wend our way through this world, sampling its pleasures, but we can never settle down. We find our place, or so we think, but then our feet get to itching, or maybe it's our hearts, for as the poet tells us, it's in our hearts that we long to go on pilgrimage.

It's not that we find what we're longing for by looking into our hearts, as some would have us believe, but that our hearts may lead us to our final destination if we listen to what they have to say. If we pay attention, we'll hear them murmur their discontent with this world and their desire for a better place.

And, believe me, there is a better place: our Father's house. Though we may not know it, our soul "yearns, even faints, for the courts of the LORD." We "cry out for the living God."[263] We're mostly home-sick, yearning for our Father and our eternal home. Everything else leaves an empty void.

Many years ago a young philosophy student told me about a tutorial in which he and his professor were discussing Thomas Aquinas's proofs for the ex-istence of God. At one point the professor, who was not a Christian, looked wistfully out of the window and murmured, "There must be a God because I miss Him so." It occurs to me thus that we may find God's presence by first noting its absence.

All through our lives God has been drawing us toward His love and away from other affections. The journey begins at birth, continues through adoles-cence into middle age, and intensifies as we get closer to our eternal home. His wooing is the source of our dissatisfaction on earth and our yearning for that elusive "something more."

He is also our satisfaction. When we come to Him, we find a companion who, unlike others, will never forsake us. He is a strong, wise, and gentle guide to our destination. His presence makes the present jour-ney lighter, less wearing, despite its peril and pain. "Good company in a journey makes the way seem shorter," said Izaac Walton.

Now that I'm getting closer to the end of my journey, I'm thinking more like a transient. I suppose it's natural. I note that Abraham first described himself as a pilgrim when he was buying a burial plot for Sarah.[264] Time and death make you think about such things.

Most of God's elderly children say the same thing: There's no home for us this side of heaven. Like John Bunyan's Pilgrim, once we've caught sight of the Celestial City we can never be content with anything less. We've found our home in God alone. Happiness is trusting in Him.[265]

"Home is behind, the world ahead," the hobbits sing as they trudge away from the Shire in *The Lord of the Rings*. For us, it's the other way around: "The world is behind, our home ahead." There are no valleys of weeping there, for He will wipe every tear from our eyes. "There will be no more death or mourning or crying or pain," for the world as we know it will have passed away.[266] That makes the present journey lighter, easier on old hearts and knees.

Put another way, it's the hope of going home that keeps me going. I can hardly wait to get there.

AGELESS DELIGHT

It is against reason to be burdensome to others, showing no amusement and acting as a wet blanket. Those without a sense of fun, who never say anything ridiculous, and are cantankerous with those who do, these are vicious, and are called grumpy and rude.[267]

—THOMAS AQUINAS

A few fortunate senior citizens go on pretty much as usual with few parts out of order. But for the majority of us, aging exacts its toll. Solomon's description of the process sums things up well:

> In old age, your body no longer serves you so
>   well.
> Muscles slacken, grip weakens, joints stiffen.
> The shades are pulled down on the world.
> You can't come and go at will. Things grind to a
>   halt.
> The hum of the household fades away.

You are wakened now by bird-song.
Hikes to the mountains are a thing of the past.
Even a stroll down the road has its terrors.
Your hair turns apple-blossom white,
Adorning a fragile and impotent matchstick
     body.[268]

The odd thing, however, is that most of us don't *feel* old. Oh, there are days when we feel every one of our years; but in general there's a vast disparity between the sight that confronts us in the mirror each morning and the young person that resides within. One of my favorite quotations from Frederick Buechner's *Godric* hangs in a place of honor over my desk and expresses my heartfelt sentiment: "Deep inside this wrecked and ravished hull there sails a young man still." I'd like to keep that positive outlook to the end.

To think of all the things we used to do in the "good old days" and can't do any more only makes a body feel worse. It's much better to poke fun at oneself rather than grumble and complain. Arthritic joints, hearing and memory loss, and failing eyesight are no fun, but we can survive them by managing to see them, among other things and despite all, as desperately funny.

There's something delightful about old folks who keep their sense of humor. They're a joy to be around. Like the eighty-year-old gardener who, when asked how old he was, replied, "I'm an octogeranium." You gotta love it! An old man with a young mind and puckish wit, the kind of person you love to be around. So much better than being a "grumpa," as one little girl described her gloomy grandfather.

Some years ago I came across a printed message by Dr. W. H. Lax, a Methodist minister who worked among the poor of London in the nineteenth century. In this message he gives wise counsel to those in their sunset years.

> The age of the body, apart from actual disease, depends upon the vital organs: the heart, lungs, and the like. These are "set" for a certain period. They may get worn out, either by fair wear and tear, or, much sooner, by unfair wear and tear. You cannot help that.
>
> But you can control the age of your mind. You can, if you face life in the right spirit, keep the mind young almost indefinitely. And remember that the mind controls the activities and energies of all the rest of the body. It is the supreme organ. If you let the mind grow old, the body will grow old also.
>
> How are you to keep the mind young? The most important thing is to cultivate a cheerful spirit, never allowing pessimism to gain the upper hand. Make up your mind to maintain a buoyant outlook on life. When the sun shines, let it shine on

you. Grey days will come, but always think of the sunny days which must assuredly follow. Hang on to your sense of humor with both hands. The older you grow, the more you will need it. Most of the neurotic wrecks one sees, and some of the mental ones, are the natural result of a morbid outlook on life.

And keep an open, active mind. You cannot keep the mind young if you persist in looking at the gloomy side, or in closing it to new ideas, muffling it up in prejudices and stifling its enthusiasms. It is losing the thrill and zest of life that makes a man old. He doesn't lose the thrill because he is old; he becomes old because he has lost the thrill. The moment a person loses his sense of wonder at the beauty of a sunset, or the glory of heroism and self-sacrifice, or the intricate markings on a butterfly's wing, or the marvels of science, he becomes old.

Humor is also a component of *joy*, which G. K. Chesterton called "the gigantic secret of the Christian . . . the dominant theme of Christian faith." Christianity, he said, "satisfies suddenly and perfectly . . . in this; that by its creed joy becomes something gigantic and sadness something special and small."[269]

In other words, *faith* leads us to holy humor.

Faith puts its trust in God's wise providence, His compassionate, kindhearted care, His unfailing love,

His promise that someday He will take us to be with Him forever. These are the infallible truths that sustain us, that enable us to rise joyfully each morning, whatever we have to face throughout the day.

Israel's prophet, Habakkuk, put it this way:

Though the cherry trees don't blossom
    and the strawberries don't ripen,
Though the apples are worm-eaten
    and the wheat fields stunted,
Though the sheep pens are sheepless
    and the cattle barns empty,
I'm singing joyful praise to God.
    I'm turning cartwheels of joy to my Savior
    God.[270]

SOUR GRAPES

Your vanity and greed and lust
Are each your portion from the dust
Of those that died, and from the tomb
Made you what you must needs become.
    —WILLIAM DEAN HOWELLS, "HEREDITY"

Some of us may reach old age saddled with sinful dispositions we've carried with us through the years. No matter what we do, we can't seem to shake them. Studies in the behavioral sciences do suggest that there may be negative psychological traits that are genetically influenced. Some individuals appear to be born with dispositions toward alcoholism, sexual aggression, erratic work habits, and other personality disorders, and may carry those dispositions with them.

The apostle Paul would agree: "Through the disobedience of the one man the many were made sinners."[271] Whether we go back to Adam or some other relative, whether we talk about major perversions or sins we think of as peccadilloes, every one of us has been cursed by an ancestor, handicapped by his wrongdoing, saddled with insecurities and sinful behaviors. Wrongdoing resides in our DNA, without our consent, demanding compliance.

It's common these days to assume that wrongdoing includes only those behaviors that are voluntary and unforced. If it can be shown that some orientation is caused rather than chosen, we render human choice irrelevant and remove that behavior from the realm of moral argument. Our ancestors made us what we have become. Our fathers have eaten sour grapes and our teeth have been set on edge.

"No," the prophet Jeremiah would say. "Whoever eats sour grapes, his *own* teeth will be set on edge." Regardless of the roots of my behavior I am morally responsible for the wrong that I do.[272]

But here's the good news: *We're not stuck.* The laws of heredity are not the highest laws. There is one higher—the law of God.

It does no good to excuse our sin, or even our inherited predispositions. The only way to rid ourselves of an evil trait is to call it what God calls it—sin—and bring it to Him for His forgiveness. He can then begin to bring about a cure.

No matter what the origin of our sin may be, it is fully forgiven. Our sin may be awful—so shameful we cannot bear to think about it. But I ask you, can any sin be so terrible that it's not included in the atonement Jesus made? John tells us that Jesus' sacrifice was not for our sins alone, but *for the sins of the entire world!*[273] Think of the sins committed in the world this past year and add to them the sins of everyone who ever lived in every generation. All those sins have been forgiven. Is yours excluded? No, because the atonement was an *infinite* sacrifice for sin, even sins we inherited from some corrupt, depraved ancestor.

And so we must bring our failed and flawed temperaments to Jesus, even though our choice to do so is nothing more than the end product of a lifetime of failure and our last resort. We may have struggled so long with our compulsions that we've given up, or given in to them. But God does not despair of us, even when we despair of ourselves. He assures us: "I will forgive [your] iniquity, and [your] sin I will remember no more."[274]

Some of us are difficult cases. Flawed by environment and indulgence, as well as heredity, our personalities resist change. We have "a hard machine to drive," C. S. Lewis would say. Yet God can take the most difficult and damaged life and gradually turn it into good. He does not leave us in ruins. He is watching over us "to build and to plant."[275]

For me that progress has been neither swift nor painless, but chaotic and subject to agonizing delay. I've made no quantum leaps, only tentative steps mingled with many hard falls. It's been a gradual thing, better seen in retrospect than in prospect. Yet for reasons only God knows, some of us may glorify Him for a time through flawed temperaments. We're so damaged that total healing awaits heaven.

If you're one of His children so afflicted, you can be assured of His promise: there will be progress. The God who started His great work in you will "keep at it and bring it to a flourishing finish on the very day Christ Jesus appears."[276]

I'm often drawn to John Donne's sonnets, for he too struggled mightily with hereditary sin. He writes,

Thou hast made me, and shall thy work decay?
Repair me now, for now mine end doth haste,
I run to death, and death meets me as fast,
And all my pleasures are like yesterday;
I dare not move my dim eyes any way,
Despair behind, and death before doth cast
Such terror, and my feeble flesh doth waste
By sin in it, which it t'wards hell doth weigh.
Only thou art above, and when towards thee
By thy leave I can look, I rise again;
But our old subtle foe so tempteth me,
That not one hour myself I can sustain;
Thy grace may wing me to prevent his art,
And thou like adamant draw mine iron heart.[277]

THE ART OF CORRECTION

We are often unable to tell people what they need to know because they want to know something else.[278]

—GEORGE MACDONALD

E very old person thinks the world is going to the dogs, I suppose, and I'm one among them; although G. K. Chesterton, I think it was, informed us that each time the world has been in crisis in the past it wasn't the world that died but the dog.

Most of our anxieties are overrated. Furthermore, I have to remind myself that it's not my job to set the world straight, even though I think I know what's wrong with it. I'm reminded of one of Flannery O'Connor's characters, Sarah Ruth, who "in addition to her other bad qualities, . . . was forever sniffing up sin."[279] I don't want to gather that reputation.

Yet every once in awhile it comes to me that I ought to say *something* to my friends about the way they're conducting their lives. A word here or a word there might help.

Correction is "a kindness," Israel's King David insisted,[280] a word that suggests an act of loving loyalty. Loyal friends will correct one another, even when it's painful and disruptive of relationships to do so. It's one of the ways we help one another grow stronger. As the proverb states, "Wounds from a friend can be trusted."[281]

David felt indebted to those who corrected him and realized how much he owed them. "Let a righteous man strike me—it is a kindness; let him rebuke me—it is oil on my head. My head will not refuse it."[282]

Not everyone appreciates correction, however. It takes grace to receive correction. Unlike David, most folks are inclined to refuse it. But if they do accept the reproof, they will find, as David did, that it does become a fragrant oil on their heads, an anointing that makes their lives a sweet aroma wherever they go. Growth in grace does not always come through rapturous moments of biblical insight and spiritual delight. Sometimes it comes through the unpleasant chiding of a friend.

It occurs to me, however, that it also takes grace to *give* correction. We can be too severe. As Job said of the verbal blows his would-be friend Elihu gave him, his "arrow inflicts an incurable wound."[283] Sometimes our efforts to heal result in harm.

Lucian, the Greek rhetorician, wrote of his mentor, Demonax: "[He] was never known to shout or be overly vehement or angry, even when he had to correct someone. He touched on offenses, but pardoned offenders, saying that one should model one's self after doctors, who treat sickness, but are not angry with the sick. He thought that to err was human, but to put the error right was divine." (Here's another example of Jesus' axiom that the sons of this age are sometimes wiser than the sons of light. Demonax anticipated by two hundred years the biblical idea that we should condemn the sin while forgiving the sinner.)

Note that Demonax did not say, "to *forgive* is divine," as Alexander Pope turned the phrase, but rather, "to *put the error right*" is divine. It's one thing to forgive an offense; it's quite another to help an offender heal. When we do so, we have aligned ourselves with God and His divine work of sanctification and have become fellow-workers with Him.

And remember, the first step in helping others is to take heed to ourselves. We're inclined to be so preoccupied with other people's faults that we fail to do justice to our own.[284] As Jesus put it, we have to take the beam out of our own eye before we consider the mote that obscures our brother's sight.

The only wisdom we can hope to acquire
Is the wisdom of humility: humility is endless.[285]

HIS STORY

Aslan seems to be at the back of all the stories.
—C. S. LEWIS

In his letter to the Galatians, Paul writes about meeting the apostle Peter for the first time. Paul says he went up to Jerusalem to "get acquainted with" Peter "and stayed with him fifteen days."[286] Paul's word, here translated "get acquainted," is the Greek word *historeo,* which means "to visit and to learn about someone."

Paul makes it clear that he and Peter did not discuss the gospel on that occasion, for Paul's perception of the good news came through direct revelation from Christ himself, and not from any of His apostles. I can't help but wonder, then, what these two men *did* talk about. We can't be sure, of course, but the text suggests that Paul asked about Peter's "history"—the story of his life.

As we age, it makes a lot of sense to reflect on our own story and, while we're about it, to look back and recall God's faithfulness, even in the midst of our troubles. It's important to think about our experiences and view them in the light of the whole of life's journey. We may then see that some event that caused us great pain also brought great blessings to us and to others.

As we reflect on the past, we can become aware of "and rely on the love God has for us."[287] We'll see that our history has been a story of that love coming upon us in stages, from birth to the present. Birth itself is a gift of the Father's love, as was the gift of new birth when we entered fully into God's love. These are but two of the many good things God has given us, sprinkled throughout our years. For all these gifts we can sing in gratitude: "Blessed is the Lord who has shown me the wonders of His love."

Thinking about the past doesn't remove the reality of our sufferings or disappointments, but it can change the way we look at them. Younger people cannot fully understand why we older folks return to the distant past, but such reflection has its place. And when it is done in prayer and thanksgiving, it can be a source of wonderment and deep healing.

I find that sleepless nights are a good time to accumulate those memories. David wrote:

> On my bed I remember you;
>> I think of you through the watches of the
>> night.
>> Because you [have been] my help.[288]

In this way we turn our memories into holy memoirs.

As I write that, I realize that the word "memoirs" has exactly the right sound to it, because it suggests a *written* account of life's accumulated memories. It's good, I think, not only to *tell* our story to others, but to *write it down* for the next generation. And perhaps someday someone will read our story and, by God's grace, make something of themselves that we could not make of ourselves, for those who come behind ought always to go beyond us.

"Don't adventures ever have an end?" asks the hobbit Bilbo. "I suppose not. Someone else always has to carry on the story."[289]

ASLEEP IN JESUS

One short sleep past, we wake eternally,
And death shall be no more; Death, thou shalt
die.

—JOHN DONNE

I have a treasured memory of family gatherings with friends when our boys were small. The children would play while the adults talked into the night. Then, weary with play, the children would curl up on a couch, or in a chair, and fall asleep.

When it was time to leave, I would gather them in my arms, carry them to the car, lay them in the back seat, and take them home. When we arrived, I would pick them up again in my arms, take them to their beds, tuck them in, kiss them goodnight, turn out the lights, and close the door. In the morning they would awaken, secure and sheltered, at home.

This has become now, in my latter years, a parable for me of the night on which we "sleep in Jesus," as Paul would say, and awaken in our eternal home—

the home that will at last heal the weariness and homesickness that has marked our days. "One short sleep past," poet John Donne wrote, and then "we wake eternally."

Sleep is an ancient metaphor for death. Poets, prophets, philosophers, and playwrights have equated sleep and death. In sleep our eyes are closed, our bodies still, our respiration so slight that we seem not to be breathing at all.

Ancient writers, in fact, referred to sleep as "a little death." The Greek poet Homer referred to sleep and death (*hypnos* and *thanatos*) as "twin brothers." Cicero said there is "nothing so like death as sleep."

While non-Christian writers referred to death as "perpetual sleep" or "everlasting sleep," however, the sacred text speaks of a "sleep" that leads to a great awakening.

The idea of death as mere sleep is alluded to in the Old Testament. Daniel promised that Yahweh will raise up those who sleep in the dust of the earth, and David refers to the same idea when he writes, "in righteousness I will see your face; when I *awake, I will be satisfied with seeing your likeness.*"[290]

The New Testament writers give the symbol its full meaning. When Lazarus died, Jesus said to His disciples, "Our friend Lazarus has fallen *asleep*; but I am going there to wake him up." Sleep was Luke's symbol for the martyrdom of Stephen, who, when he was stoned to death, dropped to his knees and "fell *asleep.*" Paul writes, "Brothers, we do not want you to be ignorant about those who fall *asleep*, or to grieve like the rest of men, who have no hope. We believe that Jesus died and rose again and so we believe that God will bring with Jesus those who have fallen *asleep* in him." And Jesus made this same reference to a grieving couple on the occasion of their little girl's death: "The child is not dead but *asleep*."[291]

Early Christians seized on the symbol of sleep as death. The catacombs in Rome, which were first constructed and used by the early Christians for burial sites, were called *koimeteria* (from which we get our word "cemetery") or "sleeping places," suggesting that the bodies of these believers were merely resting until the resurrection, a belief reflected in numerous inscriptions on sarcophagi: "He/She sleeps in Jesus."[292]

These early Christians could extract the full meaning of the metaphor because they understood that in Christ, death is *exactly* like sleep. We slumber and awaken soon after. (We're not conscious of time when we fall asleep.) Thus sleep is good and nothing to fear. Death, in fact, is heaven's cure for all of earth's ailments—"good for what ails us," as my mother used to say. Thus there is a fine irony in the disciples' comment to Jesus: "Lord, if he [Lazarus] sleeps, he will get better."[293]

But what is it that sleeps? Is it the soul? No, the symbol refers to the *body*, not the soul. The soul does not slumber until the resurrection of the body, for in eternity there is neither time nor space. This is why Paul can write with such assurance: "To be absent from the body and [in the same instant] to be present with the Lord."[294]

The Greek verb on which the noun "sleep" is based is *koimeo,* which means "to lie down." Correspondingly, the Greek word for resurrection is *anastasis,* which means "to stand up." We "lie down" in the sleep of death and "stand up" in a resurrection to life eternal.

Paul speaks of "sleeping *in Jesus,*" as though that's the key to everything. And as it turns out, it is. It's through our Lord's death and resurrection that we are delivered from fear of death, the dread with which Satan has enslaved the world.

There is great fear of dying here on earth, as evidenced by the effort expended to ignore it, avert it, or stave it off as long as possible. Think of all the industries directed to that end. But nothing works very well or for very long. Sooner or later we all perish, and that prospect can worry us a good deal, even those of us who know Jesus.

I was walking in our park some weeks ago and happened on an old fellow making his way around the track. "How's it going?" I asked in greeting. "Well," he replied, "pretty good, I guess. I'm still looking down at the grass." His point, of course, is that looking *down* is better than looking *up* at the grass, or "pushing up daisies," as we say.

The apostle Paul would disagree. He insisted that death was better than life.

> For to me, to live is Christ and to die is gain. If I am to go on living in the body, this will mean fruitful labor for me. Yet what shall I choose? I do not know! I am torn between the two: *I desire to depart and be with Christ, which is better by far.*[295]

Paul was certain that death was the best thing for him. He had no fear of what lay ahead. But occasionally even those of us in Christ give way to dread. We may be free from fear of death itself, but the process of dying is another matter entirely. "Heaven is a wonderful place, full of glory and grace," we sing, but the passage to it is fraught with uncertainty. What will our journey to the other side be like?

Some years ago I read a story about an elderly British woman who, though she lived in the Cotswolds near London, had never been to the city. The train she would have to take passed through a long, dark tunnel, and she was afraid to make that passage. One day, however, she was forced by poor health to visit a medical specialist whose office was in the city. The poor soul boarded the train and worried herself into such exhaustion that she fell asleep—and slept through the entire ordeal. When she awoke she found herself undamaged, unharmed in the city of London.

And so it is: we sleep and awaken to eternal life in our Father's house.

This is why, in the end, we have hope for our loved ones. We may grieve for our loss, but we do not grieve "like the rest of men, who have no hope. We believe that Jesus died and rose again and so we believe that *God will bring with Jesus those who have fallen asleep in him*."[296] We no more fear their absence than we fear their sleep in the evening because we know they will awaken rested, full of glorious vigor and well-being.

"The Lord gives and the Lord takes away," George MacDonald said, "but the Lord will give *again* better than ever before." We're all getting closer to that great day.

In the book of Deuteronomy we read this simple statement about the death of Moses: "Moses the servant of the Lord died there in Moab, as the Lord had said."[297] But the Hebrew text reads: "Moses died . . . *with the mouth of the Lord*." And ancient rabbis translated the phrase: "with the kiss of the Lord." When I read this, I envision God stooping over His children, tucking them in and kissing them goodnight—to awaken in His presence to His love.

John Donne has a wonderful commentary on death as sleep in one of his sonnets. He begins with his oft-quoted phrase:

Death be not proud, though some have called
    thee
Mighty and dreadful, for, thou art not so.

"Really?" we ask. "Death not dreadful?"

Donne answers that death cannot boast because it cannot kill us. Death is mere "rest and sleepe," and there is great pleasure in sleep because "much more must flow," a place to rest our weary bones.

What Good Am I?

French essayist Simone De Beauvoir, in her study of aging, writes, "The vast majority of mankind look upon the coming of old age with sorrow or dismay. It fills them with more aversion than death itself."

King David expressed his own perspective on this when he said in his old age, "Those who see me on the street flee from me. I am forgotten," like a piece of broken and discarded pottery.[298] He was "like a portent"—an ominous, unsettling sign—for aging foreshadows human loss, decline, and death.[299]

In a culture that celebrates strength and beauty more than character and wisdom, old folks are "creepy." Younger folks don't want them around. Perhaps because they are reminded that someday they too will be old and will die.

But David rejected these sentiments. His security and sense of well–being were well-grounded, not in human opinion, but in the firm foundation of God's love.

> [You are] my rock of refuge,
>> to which I can always go ...
> From birth I have relied on you;
>> you brought me forth from my mother's womb.
> I will ever [*always*] praise you.[300]

God had been faithful in the past, and He would be faithful in David's old age. Thus David continued to pray: "Do not cast me away when I am old; do not forsake me when my strength is gone." He knew that his prayer would be answered, for God had already promised His people that He would *never* leave them, that He would *never* forsake them. Even when they were "old and gray," David assured, God would be true.[301]

> Since my youth, O God, you have taught me,
>> and to this day I declare your marvelous deeds. . .
> My mouth will tell of your righteousness,
>> of your salvation all day long,

> though I know not its measure . . .
> Even when I am old and gray,
>   do not forsake me, O God,
> till I declare your power to the next generation,
>   your might to all who are to come.[302]

David had come to know God well. He had seen God's marvelous deeds, His righteousness, His power and ability to save. This was David's legacy, his gift to the next generation.

This is our legacy as well. We have essential work to do: to draw from the reservoir of wisdom we've gathered from God through the years and pass it on to the "next generation . . . to those who are to come."

I'm not talking about biblical knowledge, as such, as useful as that can be, but about a deep spiritual wisdom and discernment gained from years of friendship with God. This is the grace and beauty of spirit with which we face chemotherapy or dialysis. It is the quiet, trustful manner in which we surmount the loss of a spouse, a child, or a grandchild. It is the patience and joyful endurance, the courage and hope in God with which we deal with the impairments of old age and the ever-approaching departure from this life. This is the wisdom we can bequeath to the next generation—the wisdom that God has imparted to us.

But, you say, "I've not known God from my youth. I'm a late starter." Not to worry. Just get started.

Give yourself to worship and prayer. Put your roots down into God's Word and grow up. "Sit down alone with God's Word and in His presence open His book," John Wesley said, "and what you earn there, speak." You can learn as long as you live and thus you will always have something to say. Old dogs and old folks can learn new tricks after all.

"I create the fruit of the lips," God says.[303] Our words are like fruit, the final reason for a tree's existence. It's why we are being cultivated. Good words come from within, the final product of God's Word hidden away in our hearts. From that reservoir He will cause us to bear fruit to the end of our days.

"We're immortal," Augustine said, "until our work is done." But when that work is over, our Lord will bring us home. This was David's firm confidence:

> You will restore my life again;
> from the depths of the earth
> you will again bring me up.
> You will increase my honor
> and comfort me once again.[304]

The One who raised Jesus from the dead will raise us up to ever-expanding eternal life. There, in our Father's house, we will be welcomed with open arms, celebrated and encircled with affirming love. There, we will hear our Master announce before assembled heaven and earth: "Well done, good and faithful servant! You have been faithful with a few things; I will put you in charge of many things!"[305]

And thus our work will go on . . .

BOOKWORM

There is no frigate like a book
To take us lands away,
Nor any coursers like a page
Of prancing poetry.

This traverse may the poorest take
Without oppress of toll;
How frugal is the chariot
That bears the human soul.

     —EMILY DICKINSON

I 've been a bookworm ever since I learned how to read. My two strongest memories as a child are pick-up baseball games at the park and sitting under a gigantic willow tree in our backyard and reading until it was dark. My parents once gave me a set of bookplates that portrayed a smiling worm sticking his head out of an apple, licking his lips and saying, "As for me, give me a book!" Books were my "frigates" that took me lands away.

And I'm still a bookworm. It's almost impossible for me to sit down without picking up something to read. Among my favorite days are Saturdays when Carolyn and I haunt our local library.

Some years ago I read a short story by Argentine writer Jorge Luis Borges entitled "The Library of Babylon," in which he describes a library that contains all the books that were ever written, or will ever be written, with all editions and all possible variations of every volume. Oh, how I'd love to have a library card for such a place!

Carolyn and I *love* books, and we give away or loan out most of our books after we've read them; otherwise our libraries would take up most of the house. (C. S. Lewis once commented that those books we've loaned out are the only books we'll have in heaven. We'll have space enough there.) The exceptions are those we cherish and want to read again and again.

My reading tastes have always been more eclectic than refined, I suppose. When it comes to books, I read widely—poetry, history, theology, philosophy, mysteries and other who-done-its—although I don't read many contemporary writers (only a few to keep up with my friends). Most of all, I like authors from the past. To read these men and women is to sit in conversation with some of the greatest minds of history.

Reading engages the mind and ignites the imagination. And mental stimulation is important as we age, for our minds, like our muscles, atrophy if we don't use them. Reading can help us keep our mind nimble, flexible, and strong. Certainly there is some cognitive loss as we age, but we can learn and our minds can expand to the end of our lives. George MacDonald wrote in his last years:

> So, like bees round the flower by which they
> thrive,
> My thoughts are busy with the informing truth,
> And as I build, I feed, and grow in youth.[306]

Above all, I read the Bible. As John Wesley said, "God himself has condescended to teach the way; for this very end he came from heaven. He hath written it down in a book. O give me that book! At any price give me the book of God! I have it; here is knowledge enough for me. Let me be *homo unius libri* [a man of one book]."[307] This is my prayer as well.

I've approached the Bible in a number of ways over the years, and all have served me well at one time or another. My current method is based on a scheme as old as Jeremiah and John: I *eat* it.[308]

I take small bites—a verse, a few sentences, or at most a short paragraph. Then I think about that text for a long time. I read and re-read it, a dozen times or more, reflecting on what the Author is saying and, more importantly, what He is saying to *me*. I've found that understanding comes through patient reading and reflection; every text must be brooded over. As Mortimer Adler writes in his *How to Read a Book*: "What things would you do by yourself if your life depended on understanding something readable which at first perusal left you somewhat in the dark?"

Some sayings are hard, so I must think hard and long about their meaning. And if I ponder the Scriptures long enough, I find there's *always* something there.

The next step is prayer, which I suppose is analogous to the enzymes that break down our daily bread. We chew and then we digest.

Folks have asked me if prayer is essential to understand the Bible, and my answer is "of course," but probably for a different reason than they may think. Almost anyone can understand the *language* of the Bible, given an application of the rules we apply to normal speech. Paul does insist that those without the Spirit cannot understand the things of the Spirit of God,[309] but I believe he was referring not to the words of Scripture, but to understanding their implication for life. I have, in the past, had non-Christian professors whose insights into the biblical text were startling. It was the *meaning* of those insights, the *personal* significance of the text, the deep wisdom that touches and changes the heart that eluded them.

It's here that prayer plays a crucial role, and it's here that the Bible is radically different from other books. Prayer cannot help me determine the difference between prose and poetry, between nouns and verbs, or between commands and general observations about life. That understanding comes from thoughtful effort, not free association, intuitive flashes, or special insight. But prayer can lead me to understand the particular truth that I need for *myself.* I believe that's what Paul meant when he presented Timothy with a series of metaphors and insisted that he reflect on them, for the Lord would give insight into each one.[310] Reflection on the words of Scripture and reliance on the Spirit of God enable me to see what God wants *me* to see.

Prayer is also essential to rid my mind of pride, prejudice, and the preconceptions to which I so doggedly cling. It enables me to hear God's Word with objectivity and susceptibility, so that I can understand what's being said to my self-will, self-indulgence, and self-reliance.

Truth cannot be rationally assimilated; the process by which the Word becomes flesh and touches our heart of hearts is supra-rational—accomplished alone by prayer. It's for that reason that Paul knelt before the Father and prayed that those in Ephesus who read his words might "know" what could not otherwise be known.[311]

Finally, what we eat must be integrated into our being. It's not enough to read God's Word and leave it there. We cannot say we know any truth until we've begun to obey it. As someone has said, "To know and not to do is not to know at all."

Jeremy Taylor wrote: "Be sure to meditate so long, till you . . . get some new arguments against a sin, or some new encouragements to virtue; some spiritual strength and advantage, or else some act of prayer to God, or glorification of him." That step, the walk of obedience, is the hardest part. Here's where we need God's help, for we are utterly helpless to help ourselves.

I find encouragement in a story Russian author Leo Tolstoy told about a cobbler, Martin Avdyeeich, who lost his wife and his little child, Kapitoshka, then lost his faith and his desire to live.[312] One day an old peasant came by—a man known for his godliness—and Martin spoke to him about his despair.

"What then is a man to live for?" Avdyeeich asked.

"For God, Martin!" the old man answered.

Avdyeeich then asked: "And how must one live for God?"

"Christ hath shown us the way. Buy the Gospels and read; there you will find out how to live for God."

So Martin bought a New Testament and began to read. "And the more he read, the more clearly he understood what God wanted of him, and how it behooved him to live for God . . . And he began to measure his own life by these words. And he thought to himself . . . O Lord, help me!"

This is my beginning: to know that I am a poor

creature, utterly incapable of doing what God has asked me to do—and to ask for His help. In this way I read the Bible these days: I ponder it long and I pray, "Lord, help me!"

Obedience flows from God's love. When I know I am loved and cherished by my heavenly Father, I long to be an obedient child. These days, it is the love of Christ that compels me.[313]

THE LITTLE BIRDS OF GOD

These birds are emblems of those men that shall
Ere long possess the heavens, their all in all.
—JOHN MILTON

A leper came to Jesus one day, probably to everyone's great surprise, for lepers were banned from polite society.[314] Dr. Luke describes the man as "covered with leprosy," so he must have been afflicted with an advanced case of the disease. He was all lesions and stumps, discolored and disfigured, shocking in his ugliness, a gross caricature of what a human being is intended to be.

Leprosy was a death sentence back then. There was no earthly cure. Lepers were required to wear sackcloth and ashes, emblems of mourning. They were "cut off from the land of the living."

Of all diseases, leprosy is the only one singled out by the Law and Prophets and associated with sin. Not because leprosy was sinful, or that sin necessarily led to leprosy, but because the disease was considered a symbol of sin—sin come to the surface. If one could see sin, it was thought, it would look something like an advanced case of leprosy.[315] Furthermore, the end of leprosy is like the end of sin: death. Lepers were the walking dead: "a sepulcher, a moving grave," wrote John Milton.

This man lingered on the outskirts of the crowd, waiting for an opportunity to approach Jesus—but not too close, lest he offend. And then he made his request: "If you are willing," he said to Jesus, "you can make me clean." This plain request for healing is touching and profound in its simplicity.

Sick and troubled people normally elicited sympathy from others, but not lepers. They were considered repulsive in every way. They were, in John Milton's words, "disease-ridden men with moldy breath; unwashed men with the ways of death." Nevertheless, Jesus was "moved with compassion." He reached out to this desperate man and *hugged* him. "Hugged" is exactly the right word. "Touched," the word used by most translators, is much too tame.[316]

Did our Lord need to hug this leper? Of course He did! It meant everything in the world to the man. It was what "daughter" was to the woman with the defiling hemorrhage; what "neither do I condemn you" was to the woman caught in adultery. No one else could or would have hugged this shockingly ugly, diseased man. Only Jesus.[317]

Then Jesus spoke the words "Be clean" and "im-

mediately the leprosy left him." And with that simple, healing pronouncement the leper was clothed in
healthy flesh.

Jesus then sent the man off to the temple to show
himself to the priest and to "offer the sacrifices that
Moses commanded for your cleansing," and here's
where the story gets even better. If the man obeyed,
the priest would have located the proper procedure
and would have read these instructions, written there
in the Law for more than a thousand years.[318]

The priest was to go outside the camp to the leper,
examine him, and declare him clean. Then he was to
take two live birds in hand: one to be sacrificed, its
blood poured out into an earthen bowl; the other to be
bound into a bundle with a piece of cedar and a sprig
of hyssop (an aromatic, sponge-like plant), wrapped
together with scarlet string. After the first bird was
sacrificed, he was then to dip the living bird in the
blood in the vessel until the hyssop was saturated
with blood, sprinkle the blood seven times on the one
cleansed from leprosy, untie the bird, and set it free.

The first bird represents our Savior, washed and
pure, then slain in the earthen vessel of His humanity, His blood poured out to take away our sin and
sprinkled on the sinner to denote *eternal* forgiveness.
Or as David put it in his memorable phrase, surely
thinking of this ancient procedure, "Cleanse me with
hyssop, and I will be clean."[319] Thus we may "draw
near to God with a sincere heart in full assurance of

faith, having our hearts sprinkled to cleanse us from a guilty conscience and having our bodies washed with pure water."[320]

The second bird represents you and me—immobilized and frustrated by our guilt, our hearts beating for freedom like the wings of that frantic little bird, straining against the fetters of guilt and shame that bind us. The little bird was powerless to free itself until it was dipped in the blood of the substitute and set free—free from the entanglements of past failure and guilt, free from sin's power to oppress and subdue, free to fly home to God.

You may remember Richard Bach's *Jonathan Livingston Seagull,* that strange little book about the earnest seagull that grunted his way up to God. Bach's bird sounded good on paper—people bought the book in more ways than one—but the essential premise was wrong. We cannot take flight from our own soul-sickness. There are too many strings attached.

It is God's birds that show us how to be free. It's the only way to fly.

Behold, I fall before thy face;
My only refuge is thy grace:
No outward forms can make me clean
The leprosy lies deep within.

No bleeding bird, nor bleeding beast,
Nor hyssop branch, nor sprinkling priest,

Nor running brook, nor flood, nor sea,
Can wash the dismal stain away.

Jesus, my God, thy blood alone
Hath power sufficient to atone;
Thy blood can make me white as snow
No Jewish types could cleanse me so.

While guilt disturbs and breaks my peace,
Nor flesh nor soul hath rest or ease;
Lord, let me hear thy pard'ning voice,
And make my broken bones rejoice.

—Isaac Watts

LONELINESS

He wants not friends that hath Thy love.
—RICHARD BAXTER

Psalm 142 is a "maskil," a song to make us wise, as the title "a maskil of David" suggests.[321] David wrote this psalm while he was taking refuge in a cave when Saul was trying to kill him. When King Achish of Gath refused to help David, he fled to a cave near Adullam, a Canaanite city. Separated from family and friends, lost and unremembered, he blurted out his lament:

> Look to my right and see;
>   no one is concerned for me;
> I have no refuge;
>   no one cares for my life.[322]

Therapists tell us that we all need someone to care about us. As he wallowed in introspection and lonely solitude, David felt that no one cared for him.

David is not alone in his loneliness, of course; in his psalm we see our own loneliness. Loneliness is a human need that no number of friends can fill—an innate loneliness that is in reality a spiritual hunger, a divine restlessness, the cry of the heart for God's love. Only when we know deep down in our hearts that we are God's beloved can we see our loneliness for what it is: Our hearts are restless for the love of God.

We cannot expect that we will never again feel loneliness in this life, but God's grace starts us on the way. His love assuages our isolation and feelings of abandonment.

It's significant to me that when David made his lonely cry, God gave David no earthly friends—only himself. As David said, "It is you [alone] who know my way."[323] Only God knew where David was; only God cared.

When we are stripped of every human friend, we find ourselves enfolded in the love of God. As Richard Baxter said, "He wants not friends that hath Thy love." What a friend we have in Jesus!

And then, knowing that God is our friend, though we may still want earthly friends, we do not crave them. We can *be* a friend rather than *need* one. Instead of leaning on others, others can lean on us. "Then the righteous will gather about me," David said, "because of your goodness to me."[324]

I prayed for friends, and then I lost awhile
All sense of nearness, human and divine;
The love I leaned on failed and pierced my heart;
The hands I clung to loosed themselves from
    mine;
But while I swayed, weak, trembling and alone
The everlasting arms upheld my own.

I thank Thee, Lord, Thou wert too wise to heed
My feeble prayers, and answer as I sought,
Since these rich gifts Thy bounty has bestowed
Have brought me more than I had asked or
    thought.
Giver of good, so answer each request
 With Thine own giving, better than my best.

              —Annie Flint Johnson

RETIREMENT

Hackney'd in business, wearied at that oar,
Which thousands, once fast chain'd to, quit no
*   more,*
But which, when life at ebb runs weak and low,
All wish, or seem to wish, they could forego;
The statesman, lawyer, merchant, man of trade,
Pants for the refuge of some rural shade,
Where, all his long anxieties forgot
Amid the charms of a sequester'd spot . . .
                    —WILLIAM COWPER

In Homer's *Odyssey*, battle-weary Odysseus sets sail for Ithaca, his island home off the coast of Greece, after long years of fighting at Troy. Along the way he encounters the goddess Circe who tells him he must go to the underworld to consult the ghost of an old prophet, Teiresias, from whom he would gain wisdom for his last years on earth.

Later, on the edge of Hades, Odysseus does indeed meet the seer who instructs him: "When you get home

. . . you must take a well-made oar and carry it on and on, till you come to a country where the people have never heard of the sea and do not even mix salt with their food, nor do they know anything about ships, and oars that are as the wings of a ship. I will give you this certain token which cannot escape your notice. A wayfarer will meet you and will say it must be a winnowing shovel that you have got upon your shoulder; on this you must fix the oar in the ground."

Odysseus was to leave his oar—the sign of his lifelong vocation—in a far-off place where people had never heard of the sea or his sea-going exploits. Then, the prophet promised, "Your life shall ebb away gently when you are full of years and peace of mind, and your people will bless you."

Battle-weary Odysseus had faced adventure after adventure for years as he tried to get home. Yet though "hackney'd [bored] in business, wearied at that oar," he was still striving to find meaning in his sea-going "work." Thus, "leaving his oar in that far-off place" becomes a vivid metaphor for leaving his work behind. Only then can he "ebb away gently, "full of years and peace of mind." For most of us, however, leaving our work behind can be more difficult than it sounds.

I have a friend who, until this past summer, was a veteran pilot for a major airline. We happened to run into one another the day he reached mandatory retirement age. "Last night I made a very difficult landing in a snowstorm in Chicago with several hundred lives in my hands. To my crew and passengers I was a god!" he mused. "Today I'm no one at all."

Most retirees can identify. Retirement not only robs us of our work, it may also rob us of our self-worth, for so much of our sense of worth is tied up in what we *do*.

It's significant to me that one of the first things people say when they first meet is, "What do you do?" which is another way of saying, "*What* are you?" and thus we define one another by our vocations. I wonder how we would respond if, on meeting us, people would ask, "*Who* are you?" I'm not sure many of us would know what to say, because without our work, we don't know who we are.

It's not surprising, then, that retirement frustrates our sense of self-regard. We're no longer needed; we're not in demand. We have no colleagues to impress and no one to command or control. We're left out of the circles of power. Our advice is no longer sought. We're nobodies. As Tolkien's hobbit Merry said to Treebeard, "We always seem to have got left out of the old lists and the old stories."

But what if we view all these losses as a good thing? For losses, properly understood, become the means by which we gain more of Christ and find rest in His love for us.

Paul, who was a man of great accomplishment and reputation, wrote, "Whatever things were gain to me [in the past], those things I have counted as loss for the sake of Christ. More than that, I count all things to be loss in view of the surpassing value of knowing Christ Jesus my Lord, for whom I have suffered the loss of all things, and count them but rubbish so that I may gain Christ."[325]

There is really only one thing necessary: resting in the love of the One who is Love itself. Everything else is "rubbish," to use Paul's word—*skuballa* in Greek—a harsh word that literally means "excrement." This is Paul's measure of his losses when compared to his gain: the infinite love of Christ.

Truth be known, our vocations will never bring us complete satisfaction, no matter what we've achieved. While work is part of the created order, and God certainly does bless the work of our hands, our own efforts and anxious endeavors will never bring us the ultimate satisfaction we crave. Rest and peace come only from living in the love of God.

We should welcome retirement, for in it we're released . . .

From anxious thoughts how wealth may be
    increased,
How to secure, in some propitious hour,
The point of interest or the post of power . . .
Safe from the clamors of perverse dispute,
At least are friendly to the great pursuit [of
    God].[326]

Put another way, retirement provides an opportunity to purify our hearts. A pure heart is an undivided heart in which there is but one desire: to be loved by our Lord Jesus and to love Him in return.[327] In that love we possess the joy we sought but never found in all our work or play, and thus, like Homer's Odysseus, may ebb away gently, "full of years and peace of mind."

SCARET OF DYING

One short sleep past, we wake eternally,
And death shall be no more; Death, thou shalt
die.

—JOHN DONNE

Mary Trumbull Slosson, whose quaint but profound folktales give us a "glimpse of Joy beyond the walls of the world," writes about a little boy who was "scaret of dying."

> Once there was a boy that was dreadful scaret
> o' dyin'. Some folks is that way, you know; they
> ain't never done it to know how it feels, and they're
> scaret . . . And one day, as this boy, his name was
> Reuben . . . was settin' under a tree . . . he heerd a
> little, little bit of a voice—not squeaky, you know,
> but small and thin and soft like —and he see't was
> a posy talkin' . . . and it says, "What you cryin' for,
> Reuben? "

And he says, "'Cause I'm scaret o' dyin'," says he; "I'm dreadful scaret o' dyin'."

Well, what do you think? That posy jest laughed, the most cur'us little pinky-white laugh't was—and it says . . . "Dyin'! Scaret o' dyin'? Why, I die myself every single year o' my life."

"Die yourself!" says Reuben. "You're foolin'; you're alive this minute."

"'Course I be . . . but that's neither here nor there—I've died every year sence I can remember."

"Don't it hurt?" says the boy.

"No, it don't," says the posy; "it's real nice. You see, you get kind o' tired a-holdin' up your head straight and lookin' peart and wide awake, and tired o' the sun shinin' so hot, and the winds blowin' you to pieces, and the bees a-takin' your honey. So it's nice to feel sleepy and kind o' hang your head down, and get sleepier and sleepier, and then find you're droppin' off. Then you wake up jest't the nicest time o' year, and come up and look 'round, and—why, I like to die, I do."

April showers bring May flowers, as they say. They also bring the stirring of hope. Spring flowers, trees, and creatures are hints of heaven, for God has planned it that way. But spring alone is not enough. It may leave us with Reuben's worry: "I ain't a posy and mebbe I wouldn't come up."

Spring's hope could be an illusion. That's why T. S. Eliot, in his pre-Christian days, thought April was "the cruelest month." But "if you believe that the Son of God died and rose again," writes George MacDonald, "your whole future is full of the dawn of eternal morning, coming up beyond the hills of life, and full of such hope as the highest imagination for the poet has not a glimmer yet."

There is a truer word. Jesus said: "I am the resurrection and the life. He who believes in me will live, even though he dies; and whoever lives and believes in me will never die. Do you believe this?"[328]

It's one thing to make a bold assertion; it's another to back it up—and back it up Jesus did, by rising from the dead, "the firstfruits of those who have fallen asleep."[329]

The Son of God died and rose again, and His resurrection is the guarantee that God will bring us up and out of the ground. A thinking, feeling, remembering, recognizable part of us will live forever.

Faith means remembering Jesus' promise of eternal life and believing that it applies to us: "I go now to prepare a place for you so that *where I am you may be also.*" That means that life after death will not be totally different from the rest of our earthly journey. It will simply be another way in which God's love comes upon us, but it will be Love in all its transforming greatness. It will mean living out the thought of eternity that God has implanted in our hearts; it will mean meeting our loved ones lost through separating death; it will mean living in a world without blood, sweat, and tears; and, most of all, it will mean seeing our Lord who loves us and has given everything He has to unite us to Him forever in love.

There's another meaning I see as I think about this. Since we go around twice, we don't have to go for all the gusto here and now. We can live in broken and ruined bodies for a time; we can endure poverty and hardship for a while; we can face loneliness, heartache, and pain for a season. We don't have to have it all on this earth, for there is another world into which we will soon be welcomed. There our Savior will mend every broken piece and part of our bodies and wipe away the tears of pain. There will be "no more death or mourning or crying or pain, for the old order of things has passed away."[330]

We will say to one another, "This is what I've been waiting for all my life!" and then we'll spread our wings and fly!

THERE IS REST

I'm climbin' up the mountain, children;
Ain't got time for to stay.
Ain't nobody gonna turn me 'round,
Gonna make it to the judgment day.
—TRADITIONAL SPIRITUAL

Is it true? Must I keep climbing? Must I "make it" to the judgment day? Is there a rest for my weary efforts? There is, God assures me.

Our Lord entered into rest when He finished the work of creation. He luxuriated in what He had accomplished and "rested."[331] Every other creation day had a beginning and an end, but not the Sabbath. It is timeless, eternal. It "remains."

The Sabbath, of course, is but a symbol and therefore cannot be our final resting place. Even the rest of Canaan was not the finale, for that was a temporary, earthly rest. But God promised "another" day on which to rest, and so there "remains" a Sabbath for God's children.[332]

Where is that place of rest? Is it in heaven? Or earth? Both, I say. There is a final rest for our worn-out bodies and weary souls on ahead, but there is also rest in the here and now. "We who have believed enter [now] that rest."[333] *Today* is the day of rest. "Come to me," Jesus said, "and you will find rest for your souls."[334]

There is *the rest of salvation*: "It is finished" was His cry. I have nothing to do but believe that my salvation is complete—nothing more. I can rest assured that God will guard my faith to the end. No one can touch me, for I am held in His hands.

There is *the rest of sanctification*: the One who began a good work in us will perfect it until the day of Christ. We can rest in His forgiveness and grace and know that He is at work to bring us to completeness in the end. When we see Him, we'll be just like Him, He assures us.

There is *the rest of ministry and service*. I am God's workmanship, created to do good works that He has prepared in advance for me. He knows the way through my world and the hazards I will encounter there. He knows my heartaches and the obstacles that must be surmounted each day. I can cease from anxious scheming and striving and rest in His sufficiency.

This is not passivity or quietism. God rested from His labors on the seventh day but works today through Providence; Jesus rested in His finished work on the cross but lives to intercede for us.

No, this is not inactivity, but restful effort, relying on the work of God's omniscient, caring Son.

Thus in all things I must make every effort to enter that rest—

In simple faith to rest
that He, who knows and loves, will do the
best.[335]

So, I say, "grow old along with me, the *best* is yet to be . . ."[336]

NOTES

1. See Psalm 71:18.
2. 1 Peter 2:3 NASB
3. T. S. Eliot
4. Joseph's "coat of many colors" was actually a long-sleeved garment with stripes on the sleeves to indicate rank. He wore it to parade his importance.
5. Genesis 37:8
6. Genesis 41:51
7. Psalm 18:30
8. See Genesis 45:5; 50:20, emphasis added.
9. William Wordsworth
10. William Thackeray
11. The old philosophers—Plato, Aristotle, and Cicero, among many—tell us that beauty is a real idea that exists apart from the material world, one of three "transcendentals"—truth and goodness being the other two. The good, the true, and the beautiful lie beyond us, they say, but are essential to our being. There's a logical order to the three: Truth manifests itself as goodness, which in turn is beautiful when you see it. Our perception of the three, however, is the other way around: Beauty leads us to goodness and goodness to truth, or in Christian thought, to Truth, *i.e.*, God Himself.

12. *Kalos*, however, does appear in the New Testament and is one of Peter's favorite words: "Live such good/beautiful (*kalos*) lives among the pagans that, though they accuse you of doing wrong, they may see your good/beautiful (*kalos*) deeds and glorify God on the day he visits us." The Old Testament word *tob* enshrines the same idea, meaning both "good" and "beautiful." It is the word used to describe creation and God's assessment that it was very "good/beautiful." It is the word the Septuagint, the Greek translation of the Old Testament Scriptures, uses in the term "good (beautiful) old age."

13. *Letter to the Ephesians* 14:1

14. 1 Peter 3:4

15. Psalm 149:4, emphasis added

16. John 7:17 NKJV, emphasis added

17. Ephesians 4:18, emphasis added

18. 2 Thessalonians 2:11

19. 2 Thessalonians 2:12

20. 2 Timothy 3:8

21. C. S. Lewis, *The Magician's Nephew,* chapter 10.

22. Matthew 5:8

23. See Hebrews 11:21.

24. Isaiah 52:12

25. Ephesians 3:18–19

26. Psalm 46:10

27. Isaiah 32:17

28. Psalm 73:24

29. William Shakespeare, *The Merchant of Venice*, 2.2. 54.

30. John Bunyan, *The Pilgrim's Progress,* Part 11, 8th stage.

31. See 1 Peter 5:10.

32. See Colossians 3:4.

33. Psalm 25:7

34. John 6:37, emphasis added

35. Isaiah 55:7; Psalm 130:3–4

36. See Psalm 138:8

37. Philippians 1:6

38. Luke 7:47

39. Genesis 22:1–2. The text draws particular attention to the fact that it was "*the* God" who spoke to Abraham. The

very God who had been so good to him now delivers this awful line: "Take your *son* . . . your *only* son . . . the son you *love*" and put him to death.

40. It would be over six hundred years later that God registered His opposition to the practice of human sacrifice when He gave the Law to Moses (Leviticus 18:21; 20:2 Deuteronomy 12:31; 18:10).

41. Sarah's death came soon after (Genesis 23:1–2).

42. See Genesis 22:3–19.

43. This is the first mention of a substitutionary atonement in the Bible. The Hebrew word *tahat* clearly means "instead of."

44. Matthew 10:39

45. This story was written by my wife, Carolyn, for our grandchildren and all God's children. I couldn't resist including it.

46. Ecclesiastes 12:4

47. Psalm 59:16

48. Psalm 138:5

49. Psalm 98:1

50. Psalm 104:12, 33. The psalm begins with a catalogue of God's works and wisdom in creation, "over which" the birds of heaven hover and "lift up their voices among the branches." (The psalmist, a shrewd observer, notes correctly that singing is limited to *perching* birds.) The psalmist then responds, "[Therefore] *I* will sing praise to my God as long as I live."

51. Romans 6:23

52. The Hebrew verb, *bahal,* in 90:7 can have this connotation. (See Harris, Archer, Waltke, *Theological Wordbook of the Old Testament.*)

53. The Hebrew word translated "span" in verse 10 (NIV) is literally "pride" and refers to the prime of life.

54. Isaac Watts, "O God, Our Help in Ages Past"

55. George Herbert, "The Temple"

56. Compare 90:14 with 90:5.

57. See Acts 13:36.

58. See 2 Corinthians 5:18 NKJV.

59 Thomas Merton, journal, May 30, 1968

60 See Ephesians 2:10.

61. Malachi 4:2

62 See Psalm 77:1–4.

63. See Psalm 77:19–20 here and for the rest of the Scripture references in this chapter.

64. C. S. Lewis, *Letters to Malcolm Chiefly on Prayer*, chapter 14.

65. Isaiah 43:2

66. I'm reminded here of the character on *Saturday Night Live* who ended his monologue with the reminder: "And remember, looking good is better than being good."

67. Ephesians 2:10

68. Washington Irving, *The Sketch Book,* "The Angler."

69. Jeremy Taylor, *The Whole Works of the Right Rev. Jeremy Taylor, D.D.*, "Agenda, or Things to Be Done."

70. Zechariah 11:7–13

71. Ecclesiastes 9:14–15

72. A social worker I know commented recently that, in his opinion, the insatiable demands of those who feel "entitled" and their bitter resentment when their demands are not met, more than any other cause, produce care-giver burnout—the fatigue and depression that plague so many of his colleagues.

73. George MacDonald, *A Hidden Life and Other Poems*, "Lessons for a Child."

74. Luke 6:35, emphasis added

75. 1 Corinthians 13: 5 NKJV: "Does not behave rudely." The verb *aschemonei* means to be unmannerly" (*Lidell and Scott* Greek Lexicon).

76. William Shakespeare, *Much Ado about Nothing,* 3.5.

77. 2 Corinthians 4:16–17, emphasis added

78. Paul's word, *egkakeo* (translated "lose heart" in 2 Corinthians 4:16), means to lose one's motivation, to become discouraged, to give up. "In place of a negative expression such as 'not to give up,' it may be better . . . to use a positive equivalent, for example, 'to keep on' or 'to continue'" (Louw and Nida, *A Greek and English Lexicon of the New Testament*). Hence, my encouragement: "We can press on. . ."

79. Isaiah 60:1
80. 2 Samuel 1:23–24
81. 1 Samuel 26:20
82. Philippians 4:8
83. 1 Peter 4:8
84. Ambrose Bierce, "T.A.H."
85. Michael Leunig is a cartoonist, philosopher, poet, and artist.
86. Peter Kreeft, *The God Who Loves You*, Ignatius Press, 2004, 26, 27.
87. F. B. Meyer
88. George Matheson
89. "God of Our Life through All the Circling Years"
90. Hebrews 11:8
91. "Boll Weevil," American folksong
92. Psalm 91:1, 9
93. Psalm 90:1
94. John 21:18–19
95. Our English word *humility* comes from the Latin word *humus*, which means "ground, earth or soil," and from *humilitas* (from which we get *humiliation*), which means "nearness to the ground."
96. John 12:24
97. 1 Samuel 2:7–8
98. "What is the Sword of Damocles," ancienthistory.about.com; "Damocles," *The Columbia Encyclopedia*, Sixth Edition, Bartleby.com
99. Annie Johnson Flint
100. Psalm 10:14, emphasis added
101. Socrates' word, here translated *character,* means "direction" and refers to the trajectory of one's life toward the "Good."
102. Plato's *The Republic*, Book I.
103. Proverbs 16:31 NKJV, emphasis added
104. Thomas à Kempis, *The Imitation of Christ*, chapter 23.
105. Galatians 6:8
106. Henry Durbanville
107. Exodus 4:10
108. Exodus 4:11 *The Message*

109. 2 Corinthians 12:8–10
110. Psalm 41:1 NASB. "The word *considers* is striking, in that it usually implies giving careful thought to this person's situation, rather than perfunctory help" (Derek Kidner, *An Introduction and Commentary on Books I and II of the Psalms,* Intervarsity Press: Leicester, England, p. 161).
111. John Newton wrote on one occasion: "If, as I go home, a child has dropped a halfpenny, and if, by giving another, I can wipe away its tears, I feel I have done something. I should be glad to do greater things, but I will not neglect this."
112. Hebrews 4:16
113. It's worth noting that while David showed mercy to the weak, he received none from his enemies, nor even from his close friend (Psalm 41:4–9). We will always receive more mercy from God whom we have wronged than we will from our friends whom we have helped.
114. Henry Drummond, *The Greatest Thing in the World*
115. Albert Barnes, British politician
116. James 3:13 NKJV
117. George MacDonald states that the truly good person is one "around whose gate and garden children are unafraid to play."
118. "In a number of languages 'gentleness' is often expressed as a negation of harshness, so that 'gentleness' may often be rendered as 'not being harsh with people,' but gentleness may also be expressed in some instances in an idiomatic manner, for example, 'always speaking softly to' or 'not raising one's voice'" (Louw & Nida, *Greek-English Lexicon of the New Testament*).
119. Hebrews 5:1–2
120. Zechariah 9:9. The Greek version of the Bible uses *praus* here.
121. Matthew 11:29
122. George MacDonald, *The Diary of an Old Soul*, December 12.
123. Isaiah 40:28–31
124. Isaiah 50:4 KJV

125. George MacDonald, *The Diary of an Old Soul*, December 12:1.
126. Scott Wesley Brown, "Things."
127. Shel Silverstein, *Where the Sidewalk Ends*, "Hector the Collector."
128. Psalm 65:4
129. Psalm 73:25–28
130. Psalm 23:1 KJV
131. Ezekiel 47:1–13
132. John 7:37–38
133. See Ezekiel 47:12 and Psalm 87:7.
134. C. S. Lewis, *The Chronicles of Narnia: The Silver Chair*, one-volume edition (New York: HarperCollins Publishers), 557–558.
135. Revelation 22:17
136. Isaiah 55:1–2 NKJV
137. Lewis always depicts the atmosphere of the natural world as thick and dense. In such an environment it is difficult to think clearly and act appropriately.
138. Mark 14:61. Here Mark uses a word for *silence* that suggests both silence and peaceful calm.
139. Isaiah 53:7 NASB
140. Proverbs 15:1
141. James 3:18
142. 1 Clement 21:7
143. Read the story in 2 Samuel 15.
144. 2 Samuel 15:25–26
145. Q. 27, Heidelberg Catechism, as found on Westminster Theological Seminary website at www.wts.edu/resources/creeds/heidelberg.html.
146. Tertullian, "On Exhortation to Chastity."
147. Romans 12:2
148. Romans 12:1–2
149. I'm reminded here that leprosy is the only disease singled out by the biblical writers and linked with sin. It's not that leprosy itself was sinful, or that sin necessarily led to leprosy. Rather the disease was thought of as a *symbol* of sin—sin come to the surface. If you could see sin, it was thought, it would look exactly like leprosy.

150. John 21:15–22
151. George MacDonald, *Diary of an Old Soul,* May 16.
152. Luke 22:32
153. C. S. Lewis, *Mere Christianity* (San Francisco: Harper-Collins Edition, 2001), 101–102.
154. 2 Peter 1:5 NASB
155. Phillipians 2:13
156. Jean-Nicolas Grou (1731–1803), *Manual for Interior Souls*
157 Luke 22:32 *The Message*
158. C. S. Lewis, *Mere Christianity* (San Francisco: HarperCollins Edition, 2001), 192.
159. T. S. Eliot, *Four Quartets*, "Quartet 4: Little Gidding."
160. Psalm 131:1. The Hebrew word translated "wonderful" means "transcendent," and "includes the recognition of the limits of one's own power to conceptualize and comprehend" (Jenni-Westerman, *Theological Lexicon of the Old Testament*).
161. The church father, Ireneaus, pointed out that the chief difference between orthodoxy and heresy is that orthodoxy is rooted in paradox and mystery, while heresy is usually rooted in clarity and precision.
162. Psalm 131:2
163. Luke 10:42
164. I'm using "tolerance" here in its original meaning of "forbearance." Today, "tolerance" has a whole new set of meanings. It means, among other things, that we must tolerate every action or belief no matter how absurd or obscene it may be. We cannot be principled, nor can we have informed moral convictions these days. To do so is to be declared "intolerant," out of touch, phobic and, above all, mean-spirited.
165. Ephesians 3:18
166. John Bunyan, *The Pilgrim's Progress*, The Third Stage.
167. Sir Thomas More, *A Dialogue of Comfort Against Tribulation*, written just before he ascended Hill Difficulty—his martyrdom in 1535. The exact quotation from the original is: "I will supply you ahead of time with a store of comfort, of spiritual strengthening and consola-

tion, that you can have ready at hand, that you can resort to and lay up in your heart as an antidote against the poison of despairing dread."

168. Psalm 110:7. This is a messianic psalm, as our Lord himself explained (Matt. 22:41–46); thus the "brook" is a reference to the spiritual resource to which Jesus resorted that strengthened Him to suffer the cross and enter into His royal priesthood.

169. See Ezekiel 21:18–27.

170. Genesis 49:10, emphasis added

171 Augustine Guillard

172. This is not wistful thinking. God's justice is affirmed in the Word (e.g., Genesis 18:25). Injustice will not go unpunished. The only question regarding the existence of evil is, "How long?" (Psalm 94:3).

173. Psalm 94:3, 10, emphasis added

174. 1 Peter 4:17

175. Psalm 110:67, 71; 1 Peter 4:2

176. George Herbert, "The Storm"(language updated).

177. Job 5:17

178. The word translated "respite" in Psalm 94:13 means "to be quiet and undisturbed" or "to be at rest." The Jerusalem Bible translates it: "His mind is at peace though things are bad."

179. Romans 8:28, 29

180. Luke 14:26, emphasis added

181. Mark 8:35

182. Philippians 2:9

183. Elisabeth Elliot, *A Path through Suffering* (Ann Arbor: Servant Publications, 1990), p. 101.

184. 2 Timothy 4:6

185. Ugo Bassi, as quoted by Lilias Trotter in *Parables of the Cross.*

186. Ecclesiastes 11:7–8

187. A grist-mill is *very* loud.

188. Hebrew: "When the caperberry is no longer effective." The caperberry was thought to be an aphrodisiac.

189. See Ecclesiastes 12 here and for other references throughout the chapter.

190. "Wheel" is an allusion to the water wheel by which people in the ancient Middle East raised water from their wells and cisterns for domestic purposes or to irrigate the land. The ancients knew about the circulatory system long before William Harvey "discovered" it.
191. Jeremy Taylor, *Holy Dying*
192. George MacDonald, *Diary of an Old Soul*, January 1.
193. Malachi 4:2
194. Psalm 40:3
195. George MacDonald, *Diary of an Old Soul,* September 11.
196. 1 Peter 3:9
197. Kenneth L. Holmes, *Covered Wagon Women: Diaries and Letters from the Western Trails, 1840-1849* (University of Nebraska Press, 1995). This letter was written when the party was 200 miles from Fort Laramie, on the way to California.
198. 1 Corinthians 10:12
199. C. S. Lewis, *The Screwtape Letters*
200. Proverbs 19:15   (my translation). The Hebrew noun *'atzlah,* usually translated "laziness" suggests apathy and inertia.
201. St. Gregory, *Pastoral Care* (Paulist Press), 134.
202. Philippians 3:10
203. Philippians 3:12, emphasis added. Paul's verb, which is translated here "press on," means "to run after, to chase after, to pursue with intensity"—the same word he used to describe his relentless, uncompromising pursuit of the church: "I *persecuted* the followers of this Way to their death, arresting both men and women and throwing them into prison" (Acts 22:4, emphasis added).
204. George MacDonald, *The Diary of an Old Soul*, May 21. MacDonald is not suggesting that we must work to be saved, but that our salvation may become *indeed* new life and deliverance from sin.
205. Isaiah 53:3 *The Message*
206. Matthew 21:42
207. Psalm 118:22–23
208. Psalm 118:6
209. Read Jeremiah 27:1–15.

210. Jeremiah 27:12. Jeremiah's action was not abstract symbolism. A bronze relief from Assyria depicts naked prisoners with their necks tightly fastened in a wooden yoke.

211. You can read the record in 2 Kings 24:1–25:30.

212. Lamentations 1:14

213. C. S. Lewis learned that "the hardness of God is kinder than the softness of men, and His compulsion is our liberation" (*Surprised by Joy*).

214. Hebrews 12:7

215. 2 Corinthians 4:17

216. Hebrews 12:10

217. Jeremiah 46:28 *The Message*

218. Jeremiah 27:7

219. Psalm 96:13

220. Kazuo Ishiguo, *The Remains of the Day*— "of what remains of my day."

221. See Job 16:2; 31:35.

222. Philippians 2:3

223. C. S. Lewis, *The World's Last Night and Other Essays*, 1960.

224. Jeremy Taylor, *Holy Living and Dying*. Taylor (1613–1667) was a Church of England clergyman.

225. See 1 Peter 4:7–11 here and in the following references.

226. A phrase John Wesley is said to have often quoted to himself.

227. George MacDonald, "Faith, the Proof of the Unseen" (sermon preached June 1882).

228. Hebrews 11:1

229. Thomas Aquinas, *Summa Theologica* II, II, 112, 5

230. Hebrews 11:1 NKJV

231. See 1 John 1:1–3

232. John 20:30–31, emphasis added

233. See John 20:24–29.

234. John 20:29

235. Mark 9:24 NKJV

236. See Mark 15:34.

237. John 14:21; 7:16–17

238. George MacDonald, "Faith, the Proof of the Unseen" (sermon preached June 1882).

239. Ibid.

240. J. R. R. Tolkien, *The Lord of the Rings: The Fellowship of the Ring*, Chapter 10: "Strider."

241. 1 Samuel 16:7

242. Isaiah 53:2–3

243. Note Psalm 101:6–7 and the sort of people David befriended.

244. Ecclesiastes 7:3

245. Quoted by Henry Durbanville, *The Best Is Yet to Be* (Barbour: Edinburgh, Scotland, 1950), 38.

246. Amy Carmichael, "Where Lieth Peace?"

247. Psalm 112:4, 6

248. Acts 13:36

249. John 9:4

250. Hebrews 12:1

251. Proverbs 24:5–6

252. 1 Peter 5:8

253. In moral theory *solertia* translates into giving wise forethought to truth. Once we grasp a truth we must "imagine what we will do with it" in various circumstances.

254. Mark 14:38

255. Jeremy Taylor, *The Golden Grove*, "Agenda, or, Things to Be Done," italics added.

256. Luke 17:1, 3. The word "watch" comes from *prosecho,* which means "to be in a continuous state of readiness to learn of any future danger, need, or error, and to respond appropriately" (*Louw & Nida Greek Lexicon*).

257. John Calvin, *The Institutes of the Christian Religion*

258. "God saw all that he had made, and it was very good" (Genesis 1:31). In certain contexts the Hebrew word *tob* (good) means beautiful.

259. The question "why" can be answered with a technical or teleological explanation ("teleological" has to do with ultimate ends or purposes). For example, the question, "Why is the water in that teapot boiling?" can be answered in two ways: (1) Water molecules are held together by hydrogen bonds. As the temperature of the water increases, the energy of the individual molecules increase and they

move more and more vigorously until they break the bonds holding them to each other and turn into vapor; or (2) "I'm making a cup of tea for you."

260. George MacDonald, "Unspoken Sermons"

261. Romans 12:3, emphasis added

262. Psalm 84:5

263. Psalm 84:2

264. Genesis 23:4

265. See Psalm 84:12.

266. Revelation 21:4

267. Thomas Aquinas, *Summa of the Summa*, edited and annotated by Peter Kreeft (II-II, 148, 4, Thomas Gilby, translator).

268. Ecclesiastes 12:3–5 *The Message*

269. G. K. Chesterton, *Orthodoxy,* "Authority and the Adventurer."

270. Habakkuk 3:17–18 *The Message*

271. Romans 5:19

272. See Jeremiah 31:29–30, emphasis added.

273. See 1 John 2:2.

274. See Jeremiah 31:34 NASB.

275. Jeremiah 31:28

276. Philippians 1:6 *The Message*

277. "Adamant" as used here implies a pre-seventeenth-century meaning of a magnet or magnetic rock.

278. George MacDonald, *Lilith*, chapter 9.

279. Flannery O'Connor, *Everything That Rises Must Converge*, "Parker's Back."

280. Psalm 141:5

281. Proverbs 27:6

282. Psalm 141:5

283. Job 34:6

284. See Galatians 6:1.

285. T. S. Eliot, *Four Quartets*: "East Coker"

286. Galatians 1:11–20

287. 1 John 4:16

288. Psalm 63:6–7

289. J. R. R. Tolkien, *The Hobbit*

290. See Daniel 12:2; Psalm 17:14–15, emphasis added.

291. John 11:11; Acts 7:60; 1 Thessalonians 4:13–14; Mark 5:39, emphasis added

292. Most touching, perhaps, is a third-century epitaph on the grave of a nine-year-old child, Severa, who was "preserved in long sleep for her Maker. Her body rests here in peace until it shall rise again in God."

293. John 11:12

294. 2 Corinthians 5:8

295. Philippians 1:21–23, emphasis added

296. 1 Thessalonians 4:13, emphasis added

297. Deuteronomy 34:5

298. Psalm 31:11,12

299. Psalm 71:7. The psalm is anonymous in the English text, but I assume, as does the Septuagint, that David wrote this prayer.

300. Psalm 71:3, 6.

301. Psalm 71:9, 18. See also Deuteronomy 31:6, the passage the author of Hebrews had in mind in Hebrews 13:5.

302. Psalm 71:17, 15, 18

303. See Isaiah 57:19 NKJV.

304. Psalm 71:20–21

305. Matthew 25:21

306. George MacDonald, *The Diary of an Old Soul*, January 19.

307. Henry Moore, *The Life of the Rev. John Wesley*

308. I'm indebted to Eugene H. Peterson and his *Eat This Book* for this reminder.

309. See 1 Corinthians 2:14.

310. See 2 Timothy 2:7.

311. See Ephesians 3:19.

312. Leo Tolstoy, "Where Love Is, There God Is Also"

313. See 2 Corinthians 5:14.

314. See Luke 5:12–14.

315. Miriam (Numbers 12), Uzziah (2 Chronicles 26:16–23), and Gehazi (2 Kings 5:20–27) were punished by leprosy to symbolize the horrific consequences of their vice, or so I believe. Miriam's complaints, Uzziah's pride, Gehazi's

. . . .

materialism seemed small matters, but were in fact as ugly and as loathsome as leprosy.

316. The Greek verb *haptomai* means "to grasp, to take hold of." ("Do not hold on to me," John 20:17.) One ancient version says Jesus reached out his "hands," perhaps enshrining a memory of this event.

317. By touching the unclean leper, Jesus incurred the man's "uncleanness," taking it upon himself (Leviticus 5:3). Jerome translates Isaiah 53:4: "We considered Him a leper, as it were."

318. See Leviticus 14:1–9.

319. Psalm 51:7

320. Hebrews 10:22

321. The word *maskil* carries the idea of truth that leads us to act wisely. The root noun *sekel* is often used for "success," which gives us some idea of what it means to be "successful."

322. Psalm 142:4

323. Psalm 142:3

324. Psalm 142:7

325. Philippians 3:7–8 NASB

326. William Cowper, "Retirement"

327. See David's prayer in Psalm 86:11.

328. John 11:25–26

329. 1 Corinthians 15:20

330. Revelation 21:4

331. Genesis 2:2

332. Hebrews 4:8–9

333. Hebrews 4:3. The verb "enter" is in the present tense and indicates a *present* reality.

334. See Matthew 11:28–30.

335. J. Danson Smith as quoted in L. B. Cowman, *Streams in the Desert*.

336. Robert Browning, "Rabbi Ben Ezra"

Note to the Reader

The publisher invites you to share your response to the message of this book by writing Discovery House Publishers, P.O. Box 3566, Grand Rapids, MI 49501, U.S.A. For information about other Discovery House books, music, videos, or DVDs, contact us at the same address or call 1-800-653-8333. Find us on the Internet at http://www.dhp.org/ or send e-mail to books@dhp.org.